BADMINTON

Steps to Success

Tony Grice, EdD
Hardin-Simmons University
Abilene, Texas

Human Kinetics

Library of Congress Cataloging-in-Publication Data

Grice, Tony.
  Badminton : steps to success / Tony Grice.
    p. cm. -- (Steps to success activity series)
  ISBN 0-87322-613-5
    1. Badminton (Game) I. Title. II. Series.
  GV1007.G72 1996
  796.34'5--dc20
                                         95-44484
                                           CIP

ISBN: 0-87322-613-5

Developmental Editor: Julia Anderson; **Assistant Editor:** Jacqueline Eaton Blakley; **Editorial Assistant:** Coree Schutter; **Copyeditor:** Denelle Eknes; **Proofreader:** Myla Smith; **Typesetter:** Kathy Fuoss; **Layout Artist:** Tara Welsch; **Text Designer:** Keith Blomberg; **Cover Designer:** Jack Davis; **Photographer (cover):** Wilmer Zehr; **Illustrator:** Patrick Griffin; **Mac Illustrator:** Jennifer Delmotte; **Printer:** Versa Press

Instructional Designer for the Steps to Success Activity Series: Joan N. Vickers, EdD, University of Calgary, Calgary, Alberta, Canada

Human Kinetics books are available at special discounts for bulk purchase. Special editions or book excerpts can also be created to specification. For details, contact the Special Sales Manager at Human Kinetics.

Printed in the United States of America   10 9 8 7 6 5 4 3 2 1

Human Kinetics
P.O. Box 5076, Champaign, IL 61825-5076
1-800-747-4457
http://www.hkusa.com

Canada: Human Kinetics, Box 24040,
Windsor, ON N8Y 4Y9
1-800-465-7301 (in Canada only)
humank@hkcanada.com

Europe: Human Kinetics,
P.O. Box IW14, Leeds LS16 6TR, United Kingdom
(44) 1132 781708
humank@hkeurope.com

Australia: Human Kinetics, 2 Ingrid Street,
Clapham 5062, South Australia
(08) 371 3755
humank@hkaustralia.com

New Zealand: Human Kinetics, P.O. Box 105-231, Auckland 1
(09) 523 3462
humank@hknewz.com

CONTENTS

Preface   v

The Steps to Success Staircase   vii

The Game of Badminton   1

Step 1 Ready to Play: Racket Handling and Footwork   7

Step 2 Serves: Long, Short, and In Between   22

Step 3 Overhead Strokes: Forehand and Backhand   34

Step 4 Clear: High and Deep   47

Step 5 Drop Shot: Low and Slow   60

Step 6 Smash: Fast and Steep   72

Step 7 Drive: Flat and Sidearm   83

Step 8 Around the Head Stroke: Quick and Flexible   94

Step 9 Singles' Play: Fitness and Patience   105

Step 10 Doubles' Play: Rotation and Teamwork   117

Rating Your Progress   131

Glossary   135

Suggested Readings   139

About the Author   141

PREFACE

I wrote this book to accomplish several goals. First, it has given me the opportunity to describe, demonstrate, and analyze my style of teaching and playing badminton. It is a book for players at all skill levels; for classes offered in high schools, colleges, clubs, and recreational programs; or for individuals who are learning to play on their own. It is a step-by-step process designed as a manual to teach yourself the game of badminton.

This is also a book for people who have played some badminton before. *Badminton: Steps to Success* will help you examine your game and make corrections where you need them. The emphasis on fundamentals and strategy will allow you to analyze what you are doing on the badminton court. This book will be helpful in learning new skills, evaluating old skills, and improving what you are already doing.

If you want to reach the next level, you must read, ask questions, observe, imitate more experienced players, and most of all, practice and play badminton. *Badminton: Steps to Success* provides the recipe for success. The only other ingredients you need to add are your talent, desire, and personality. I hope this step-by-step process helps you accomplish your goals and have fun as well.

The 10 steps in this book allow you to move from the basic skills into gamelike situations. There are more than 80 drills in this book to help you improve your skills, practice effectively, and record your progress. Suggested ways to increase or decrease the difficulty of the drills let you self-pace your progress to match your ability level. The sections entitled "Success Stoppers" identify typical problems experienced by players learning badminton and provide suggestions for correcting those problems. You can apply the suggestions either during practice or during a game.

The 10 steps follow a learning sequence that I have developed over a long playing and teaching career. Each step prepares you for the next one and moves you closer to becoming the best badminton player you can be. Racket-handling skills and footwork precede learning to serve, and are followed by the forehand and backhand overhead strokes. These basic skills are the foundation for more sophisticated strokes like the clear and drop shots, the smash, drive, and around the head stroke. Strategies for singles' and doubles' play are also highlighted.

I hope this book will promote the game of badminton to new heights in the United States. Badminton is a wonderful sport and a game for all ages, truly a lifetime sport. It is great exercise and fun to play. As a new Olympic sport as well as an extremely popular sport worldwide, I believe that badminton has a tremendous future.

I want to thank Human Kinetics for the opportunity to share my badminton experiences with others. I particularly want to thank two ladies who were instrumental in introducing the game of badminton to me, Elma Roane and Virginia Anderson of Memphis, Tennessee and Memphis State University, for all the lessons I have learned from them. Dr. Charles "Red" Thomas and Northwestern State University of Louisiana also provided support for me in badminton and unique opportunities to learn. I am grateful to Hardin-Simmons University for its continued assistance and support. I also thank the United States Badminton Association for its cooperation and promotion of badminton. A special thanks to Bob Roadcap for his interest and participation in badminton. And finally, I express special appreciation to Kristen Grice for her encouragement and understanding of my interest as a player, coach, teacher, and writer.

THE STEPS TO SUCCESS STAIRCASE

Get ready to climb a staircase—one that will lead you to become a more skillful badminton player. You cannot leap to the top; you get there by climbing one step at a time. Each of the 10 steps you will take is an easy transition from the one before. The first few steps of the staircase provide a foundation—a basic understanding of the fundamental skills and techniques. As you progress, you will learn the ingredients you need to experience success on the badminton court. You will learn to combine the proper stroke production with game tactics during play to begin to make instinctive and accurate decisions in game situations. As you near the top of the staircase, your climb will become easier, and you'll find that you have developed confidence in your badminton abilities that will ensure further improvement and make playing the game more enjoyable.

To prepare to become a good climber, familiarize yourself with this section and "The Game of Badminton" section for an orientation and to understand how to set up your practice sessions around the steps.

Follow the same sequence each step (chapter) of the way.

1. Read the explanation of what the step covers, why the step is important, and how to execute or perform the step's focus, which may be a basic skill, concept, tactic, or combination of the three.

2. Follow the numbered illustrations in the "Keys to Success" that show exactly how to position your body to execute each basic skill successfully. There are three parts to each skill: preparation (getting into a starting position), execution (performing the skill), and follow-through (reaching a finish position or following through to starting position).

3. Look over the descriptions in the "Success Stoppers" section of common errors and the recommendations for how to correct them.

4. The drills help you improve your skills through repetition and purposeful practice. Read the directions and the "Success Goal" for each drill. Practice accordingly and record your scores in the blank. Compare your score with the "Success Goal" for the drill. You need to meet the "Success Goal" of each drill before moving to the next one because the drills are arranged in an easy-to-difficult progression. This sequence is designed specifically to help you achieve continual success. Pace yourself by adjusting the drills to either decrease or increase the difficulty, depending on which best fits your ability.

5. When you can reach all the "Success Goals" for one step, you are ready for a qualified observer, such as your teacher, coach, or trained partner, to evaluate your basic skill technique against the "Keys to Success Checklist." This is a qualitative evaluation of your basic technique or form, because using correct form can enhance your performance.

6. Repeat these procedures for each of the 10 "Steps to Success." Then rate yourself according to the directions in the "Rating Your Progress" section.

Good luck on your step-by-step journey to developing your badminton skills, building confidence, experiencing success, and having fun.

KEY

‑ ‑ ‑ ‑ ‑ → = path of player   ▬ = target area

————→ = path of bird   1, 2, 3 = order of hits

A, B, C, D = players

THE GAME OF BADMINTON

Badminton is one of the most popular sports in the world. It appeals to all age groups and various skill levels, and men and women may play it indoors or outdoors for recreation as well as competition. The shuttlecock does not bounce and must be played in the air, thus making a fast game requiring quick reflexes and some degree of fitness. The badminton participant may also learn and appreciate the benefits of playing badminton socially, recreationally, and psychologically.

Badminton is a sport played over a net using rackets and shuttles with stroking techniques that vary from relatively slow to quick and deceptive movements. Indeed, shots during a rally may vary from extremes of 1 mile per hour on a drop shot to over 200 miles per hour on a smash. When played by experts, it is considered to be the fastest court game in the world. In a recent United States Open men's doubles final match, one rally consisted of 89 shots, but lasted only one minute. A shot passed over the net every half second! However, both singles' and doubles' play may be controlled to meet individual needs and abilities for physical activity throughout your life.

History of Badminton

Apparently several games were forerunners of modern badminton, but its exact origin is unknown. Records describe a game with wooden paddles and a shuttlecock being played in ancient China, on the royal court of England in the twelfth century, in Poland in the early eighteenth century, and in India later in the nineteenth century. A game called "battledore and shuttlecock" involved hitting a shuttlecock with a wooden paddle known as a bat or "batedor" and was played in Europe between the eleventh and fourteenth centuries. The participants were required to keep the shuttle in play as long as possible.

Battledore and shuttlecock was played in a great hall called Badminton House in Gloucestershire, England during the 1860s, and the name badminton was soon substituted for battledore and shuttlecock. The playing area of the hall was an hourglass shape, narrower in the middle than at the two ends. This suggested the need for playing the shuttle at a minimum height to keep the rally going. Badminton was played on this odd-shaped court until 1901. A string was added across the middle of the hall to make a rudimentary net. The original rules for badminton were standardized in 1887 and later revised in both 1895 and 1905. These rules still govern the sport today with only minor changes.

Badminton Today

Today, badminton is sanctioned by the International Badminton Federation (I.B.F.) worldwide. Nine member nations founded the I.B.F. in 1934. As of 1993, the I.B.F. has grown to over 120 national organizations in as many countries. Major I.B.F.-sanctioned events are the Men's World Team Badminton Championships for the Thomas Cup; the Ladies' World Team Championships for the Uber Cup; the World Individual Championships; the World Mixed Doubles Championship for the Sudirman Cup; and the World Grand Prix Finals.

The Thomas Cup for men and the Uber Cup for women are the most prestigious world badminton competitions and are held in conjunction with each other. Both are organized on a two-year cycle in the even years. Players compete for the World Individual Championships in the odd-numbered years and for the Thomas Cup and the Uber Cup Championships in the even-numbered years. The World Mixed Doubles Championship or Sudirman Cup began in Jakarta, Indonesia in 1989, and it coincides with the World Individual Championships. The major tournaments of the world make up the World Grand Prix Series. Players win points by competing in each tournament, and those accumulating the most points are invited to compete in the World Grand Prix Finals at the end of the year.

Badminton has been relatively unknown and unappreciated in the United States. Following its introduction in New York in 1878, the sport developed slowly. The American Badminton Association (A.B.A.), the first national organization in the United States, was formed in 1936. The A.B.A. held the first U.S. National Championships in Chicago in 1937 and the first national junior tournament in 1947. The U.S. men's team played very well throughout the fifties, making the final round of the Thomas Cup several times. The United States' women dominated Uber Cup competition from 1957 through 1966. The first national intercollegiate championship was held in 1970. Interest and money in professional sports increased geometrically during the 1970s, but the general public's perception of badminton as a slow-paced, leisurely game was and is a misconception.

In recent years, interest has increased substantially. The A.B.A. was reorganized in 1977 and became the United States Badminton Association (U.S.B.A.). In 1985, badminton was adopted as a full medal sport for the Olympic Games of 1992 held in Barcelona, Spain. Badminton was a demonstration sport in the 1988 Olympics in Seoul, Korea. The inclusion of badminton as an Olympic sport encourages optimism for its future popularity, recognition, and success. The U.S.B.A. is currently the National Governing Body (N.G.B.) representing badminton in the United States Olympic Committee (U.S.O.C.).

Currently, the best players in the world come from China, Europe, Korea, Malaysia, and Indonesia. Indonesian players won both men's and women's singles and men's doubles at the 1992 Olympics. Indonesia also won four of the five events at the 1994 World Championships. Badminton is presently the number one sport in Great Britain. The total number of registered badminton players in England is almost two million. The I.B.F. will increase to a projected 150 member nations by the 1996 Olympics in Atlanta. Prize money for the World Grand Prix Series and Final was over $4 million in 1993 and 1994. The immediate future for both professional and amateur badminton appears to be very bright.

If you are interested in becoming more involved in badminton, join the United States Badminton Association by writing to One Olympic Plaza, Colorado Springs, Colorado 80909 or call (719) 578-4808.

Playing the Game and Keeping Score

Badminton scoring is similar to volleyball, in that you can only score when you are serving. You decide who is serving first by the toss. This can be a coin toss, a spin of the racket, or a toss and hit of the bird into the air to see toward whom it points when it lands. If you win the toss, you may choose to serve, to receive, or to choose the side of the court that you wish to start on. Whichever choice you make, your opponent gets to choose from the remaining options. Both opponents begin the game by serving from the right court with zero or "love-all." Anytime you are serving from the court in which you started, your score should be even. An illegal serve results in loss of serve.

Make the serve diagonally across to your opponent. The feet of the server must be in the proper court and in contact with the floor until the serve is made. When the receiver is ready, the server has only one attempt to put the shuttle into play with an underhand (below the waist) serve. The receiver can stand anywhere in the proper court, but must keep both feet in contact with the floor until the serve is delivered. The receiver is considered to have been ready if an attempt is made to hit the serve. After each rally or exchange, the server initiates the serve from the appropriate side depending on whether his score is odd or even. The score should always be announced before each service with the server's score given first. If a serve hits the top of the net and continues into the proper court, it is legal and play continues.

In singles, the first serve is always made from the right side. This is because the server's score is zero, which is an even number. Anytime after the beginning of the game that the server's score is even, the service is delivered from the right side (2, 4, 6, 8, and so on). If a point is made, the server serves from the left side, which is odd (1, 3, 5, 7, and so on). Your score dictates which side you serve from. The service court in singles' play is long and narrow. The side alley is out of bounds; the back alley is in bounds or good. The serve must carry past the short service line, which is 6.5 feet from the net, and must not carry beyond the back boundary line. The lines are considered part of the court and in bounds. A bird that lands on a line is considered to be good. Read the chapter entitled "Singles' Play" to learn the strategy involved in returning the singles' serve and winning the singles' rally.

In doubles, the first serve is always made from the right side. This is because the serving team's score is zero, which is an even number. One partner starts on the right side and one partner starts on the left side. Where you start is your even court. Anytime a team's score is even, both partners should be on the side on which they started. If the score is odd, partners should be opposite of where they started. If a point is made, the server changes courts and serves diagonally across to the other side. Your score dictates which side you serve from. The first serve is always from the right side when the service comes to you after your opponents have lost their serve. If one partner loses her serve, it is sometimes referred to as "one hand down." If both partners lose their serves, it is called "two hands down," service over, or side out. Your opponents now have the chance to serve and attempt to make points. The only exception to this rule is the initial serve of the game. The team that serves first begins the game with one hand down. They get only one serve on the initial serve of any new game. Just as in singles, all doubles' games are played to 15 points. The service court in doubles' play is short and fat. The side alley is now in bounds and the back alley is out of bounds on the serve. However, once the bird is in play, the back alley is good.

The serve must carry past the short service line and must not carry beyond the doubles' long service line. Step 10 explains strategies involved in returning the doubles' serve and winning the doubles' rally.

Games normally are played to 15 points in all events except women's singles, which is played to 11. A method of extending a tie game that is peculiar to badminton is the concept of *setting*. There are two opportunities of setting in any game. During a 15-point game, if the score reaches 13-all, the game may be set or extended. Instead of playing the normal 2 additional points to 15, the person or team who reached 13 first has the option of setting the game to 18, or 5 additional points. When this occurs, the first one to 18 or 5 wins the game. The second opportunity occurs at 14-all. Instead of playing the one additional point, the player or team that reached 14 first has the option of setting the game to 17, or 3 additional points. The first player or team to 17 wins the game. In neither case does one have to win by 2 points. This concept allows the receiving player more room for error and provides more opportunities to get the serve back. You may only set the game one time.

Eleven-point games provide similar opportunities to extend a tie game. However, the option to set occurs at 9-all or 10-all. In both cases, the game will be extended by 1 additional point to 12. That is, at 9-all, 3 additional points may be played. At 10-all, 2 additional points may be played. Again this takes away some of the server's advantage. If the receiver chooses not to set the game, the game will continue until someone reaches 15 or 11.

In summary, you win the rally and a point if you are serving when your opponent

- fails in attempting to return a legal serve;
- hits the shuttle outside the proper boundary lines;
- hits the shuttle into the net;
- hits the shuttle two or more times on a return;
- touches the net with her body or racket while in play;
- lets the shuttle hit the floor inside the court;
- deliberately carries or catches the bird on the racket;
- does anything to hinder or interfere with your return;
- encroaches under the net with his feet, body, or racket;
- reaches over the net to hit a return;
- touches the bird with anything other than her racket; or
- fails to keep both feet in contact with floor while serving or receiving.

Any point that has to be replayed is called a *let*. These should occur very rarely and are usually the result of some outside interference.

The badminton court for singles' play is 44 feet long and 17 feet wide (see Diagram 1), long and narrow. The court for doubles' play is 44 feet long and 20 feet wide. The net should be 5 feet and 1 inch at the net poles, sloping to 5 feet at the top, center of the net. There is no official or standardized surface for badminton courts. A court may be indoors or outdoors; it may be concrete, asphalt, clay, grass, synthetic, or wood. However, most competitive badminton is played indoors, and because of the existing hardwood floors available in most college and school gymnasiums, wood is the most often used surface.

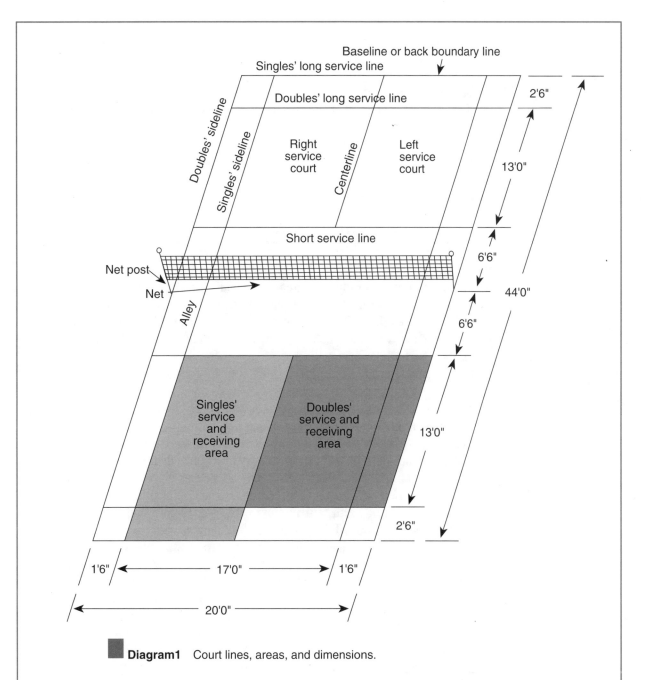

Baseline or back boundary line
Singles' long service line
Doubles' long service line
Doubles' sideline
Singles' sideline
Right service court
Centerline
Left service court
Short service line
Net post
Net
Alley
Singles' service and receiving area
Doubles' service and receiving area

2'6"
13'0"
6'6"
44'0"
6'6"
13'0"
2'6"
1'6"
17'0"
1'6"
20'0"

Diagram 1   Court lines, areas, and dimensions.

Equipment

The cost and quality of what you wear, what you play with, and where you play varies greatly. Shorts, shirt, tennis shoes, or court shoes and socks are recommended, with a warm-up suit in cooler weather. White reflects heat better than darker colors and is cooler. Many players wear nylon, cycling shorts, or a cotton pant liner under their shorts for support and comfort. In addition, headbands, wristbands, and towels help keep perspiration from the face, eyes, and hands. A soft, leather glove is often used to provide a better grip and cushion the hand.

Newer, lighter rackets of boron, carbon, or graphite are often one piece in design and can be made of varying degrees of stiffness. There are also wide-body and oversize rackets for less air resistance and less torque. Strings are usually nylon or synthetic gut.

A good medium-priced racket is suggested at first. It is a good idea to hit with several types of rackets. If possible, borrow one from a friend. Some stores have demonstration models that they will allow you to try. Compare and choose the racket that feels the most comfortable to you.

Warming Up and Cooling Down

The most common but least effective way to warm up is rallying over the net. Without proper warm-up, the chance of injury is greater. A good warm-up should prepare you for strenuous activity without tiring you out. A general warm-up to increase your blood circulation might begin with light calisthenics or jogging around the court. You may combine running toward the net with backpedaling away from the net, along with shuffling sideways across the court while facing the net. After you have warmed your muscles and increased your circulation, you are ready to stretch your upper body, shoulders, back, and legs. You should go through a series of basic stretches slowly with little or no bouncing before playing. Research indicates that passive or static stretching is better for you and less likely to cause injury. You should hold each stretch for approximately 20 seconds.

Now you are ready to hit. Include in your warm-up about 5 to 10 minutes of easy hitting while practicing specific shots. Start in the midcourt with controlled, easy exchanges with your practice partner or opponent. Begin with overhead strokes on both the forehand and backhand sides to further warm up and stretch your shoulders, upper body, and legs. Next, move laterally, reaching to hit returns from either side of your body. Move from the backcourt near the baseline toward the net, alternating returns with your partner to move each other from frontcourt to backcourt. Alternate roles with your partner to practice clears, drop shots, and smashes. Practice drop shots from backcourt, while your partner returns them with underhand clears from up at the net.

After strenuous activity, you should cool down by allowing your body to gradually return to a normal pace. Walk the perimeter of your court for about 5 minutes or until your heart rate returns to around 100 beats per minute. Then repeat your stretching exercises while you are still warm. This cooldown helps to get rid of lactic acid built up during vigorous exercise and helps to prevent muscle soreness.

Badminton requires a certain level of fitness. In close matches, fitness usually is a factor in the outcome. Important considerations in your conditioning program are exercise, a sound diet, adequate sleep, rest, and practice.

STEP 1

READY TO PLAY: RACKET HANDLING AND FOOTWORK

"Float like a butterfly, sting like a bee" is an often-quoted line from former heavyweight boxing champion Muhammad Ali. It is an excellent description of how you need to move and hit in badminton play. Good footwork is concerned with reaching the bird as fast as possible with as little effort as possible, like the butterfly. It gets you into the best position to execute your shots or sting like a bee, while maintaining good balance and body control.

The purpose of this step is to start getting your hands and feet ready to execute quickly and efficiently. The various ways to hold your racket for a forehand, backhand, serve, and other shots will be discussed and illustrated later. In order for racket handling and footwork to become a habit, practice and repetition along with some additional thought during play are required.

Why Is Racket Handling Important?

Getting accustomed to the feel and weight of the racket prepares you to handle it comfortably during play. You learn or sense how far away the racket is from your body. This is the beginning of your hand-eye-racket coordination, which is essential in making contact with the bird. Beginning players often swing and miss the bird completely. This sense of feel or timing plays a very important role in your stroke production. Beginners may hit the shuttle with the frame or make contact somewhere other than

the center of the strings, but practice in hitting, blocking, bouncing, or even picking up the shuttle with your racket reinforces the way the racket feels and enhances your racket-handling skill. Try to improve your hand-eye coordination by creating your own racket-handling drill, or use those suggested in this step.

How to Handle the Racket

Good badminton players constantly move the racket around in their hands. The lighter racket makes it possible to effectively use wrist action initiated by forearm rotation, and therefore, you can manipulate the racket at a greater speed. In addition to the lighter racket, the lightness of the shuttle makes possible greater use of the wrist without loss of control. Your racket head may be moving at a terrific speed as you throw it out to meet the shuttle. This indicates that you need a firm grip at contact. However, it is essential not to grip your racket too tightly. Ideally, your grip in badminton should provide flexible and effortless movement of the wrist and a comfortable and secure grip with your dominant hand. To learn the various parts of a badminton racket, see Figure 1.1.

Your forehand grip is sometimes referred to as either the pistol or handshake grip. You should slide the racket into your hand as if shaking hands with it. Your right forefinger is slightly apart from the other fingers providing the trigger finger effect as in holding a pistol. If your racket is perpendicular to the

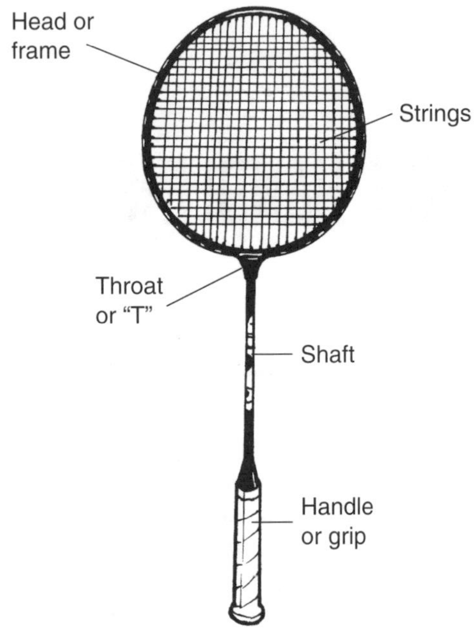

Figure 1.1   Parts of the racket.

floor, then you are holding the racket correctly. It is almost identical to the Eastern forehand grip in tennis. For the backhand, the only change is that your thumb is straight up and down on the top, left-hand bevel of your handle instead of wrapped around it. The advantage of this handshake grip is that it enables you to hit all shots without changing your grip. The thumb-up grip provides added support and leverage for all your backhand strokes. Figure 1.2 illustrates your handshake grip.

FIGURE 1.2   **KEYS TO SUCCESS**

HANDLING THE RACKET
Execution

1. Shake hands with racket ___
2. Reach for shuttle with arm extended ___
3. Snap racket through with emphasis on forearm rotation ___

Why Is the Ready Position Important?

An alert, ready position enables you to move quickly as soon as you determine the direction of your opponent's return. Your feet are square and spread about shoulder width with your knees slightly bent. Your weight is on the balls of your feet. Hold the racket head up, in front of your body slightly on the backhand side. Hold your racket with a handshake or pistol grip.

Players vary this ready position to meet their own style and needs. Some players stagger their feet slightly to be ready to move to the side, to the net, or to the backcourt more quickly from the centercourt position. This is necessary when you are waiting to receive the serve because you must have your feet in a staggered or up and back position to anticipate a long, short, flick, or driven serve. Your racket is usually held slightly higher to react more quickly to a flick or driven serve, or a poor serve.

How to Get Ready for Shots

When you are in the ready position, you should be watching the bird leave your opponent's racket and expecting the bird to come back over the net to your side of the court every time. Because the shuttle rarely comes to you during a rally, most shots are hit on the run. One way to get there is to take small, bouncy steps, shuffling or sliding into position to hit. You should try to recover to midcourt after every return. However, stop where you are before your opponent's return even if it is not possible to get completely back to center court. It is essential not to be moving when your opponent hits the shuttle. It will be easier to go farther from a standstill than changing direction while moving.

As your opponent gets ready to hit, watch his or her racket. Focus on the bird, and wait until you are sure of the direction the shuttle is traveling before moving (see Figure 1.3a). Do not guess or anticipate too soon. From the ready position, as soon as you determine the direction of the return, pivot, reach with the dominant foot, shuffle or take a step-close-step or skipping action. You should keep your feet close to the floor and cross your feet over when you move to the backhand, but not the forehand side (see Figure 1.3b).

When you go to the net, your dominant leg is normally leading and pushes off to return to midcourt (see Figure 1.3c). However, if you also bring the nondominant foot forward and plant it near the dominant foot, then lean backward, the subsequent push off with both legs greatly assists in changing direction and propelling you back to center court even faster.

FIGURE 1.3 **KEYS TO SUCCESS**

READY POSITION AND FOOTWORK

Preparation

1. Feet shoulder width apart __
2. Toes straight __
3. Feet square or slightly staggered __
4. Knees flexed __
5. Put weight on balls of feet __
6. Hold racket up __
7. Handshake or pistol grip __
8. Keep your eyes on bird __

Execution

1. See bird and opponent __
2. Pivot on nondominant foot __
3. Lead with dominant foot __
4. Reach with dominant arm and leg __
5. Step-close-step or shuffle feet __
6. Use crossover step only on backhand __

Follow-Through

1. Push off lead foot __
2. Push off both feet __
3. Propel yourself back to midcourt __
4. Repeat three-step pattern in reverse on backhand __
5. Keep your balance __

RACKET HANDLING AND FOOTWORK SUCCESS STOPPERS

Lack of awareness or practice usually causes problems with racket handling, achieving the ready position, and movement on the court. Very few players emphasize this part of their game. Your racket should become an extension of your hand, with your grip comfortable and firm without any need to think about it. You should consistently recover or fall back to your centercourt position instinctively. Americans have less experience in foot-related activities, such as soccer and ballet. You should spend some time practicing and repeating drills to develop speed and efficient movement on the court.

Error	Correction
1. You don't have enough time to recover.	1. Begin in the ready position. Recover to midcourt after each shot.
2. You don't have enough time to get to the bird.	2. Return quickly to center court after each shot. Stop before your opponent hits his return.
3. Your dominant leg gets very tired from going up to the net.	3. Divide the workload evenly between the two legs by pulling the trailing leg up under the body and pushing back with both legs.
4. The bird gets behind you.	4. Keep your racket up and move quickly as soon as you determine the direction of your opponent's return.
5. You don't have enough time to change or adjust your grip.	5. Use a handshake or pistol grip, which allows you to hit your backhand with only a slight change from your forehand. For the backhand, the only change is that your thumb is straight up and down on the top, left-hand bevel of the handle instead of wrapped around it.
6. You get fooled and are caught moving before your opponent's racket contacts the bird.	6. Focus on the bird during your opponent's stroke as long as possible. Try to see the shot hit your opponent's racket and don't focus on your opponent's upper body movements.
7. You experience inconsistent shots or rallies caused by failure to recover to your ready position.	7. Get in good shape so you can move quickly and effortlessly. Fatigue often causes inconsistency.

RACKET HANDLING AND FOOTWORK

DRILLS

1. Handshake

Take turns with your partner, shaking hands with the racket handle to learn the pistol grip. Start with the racket on edge. Grasp the racket handle as if you were shaking hands with it. Slide the racket into your hand with your forefinger slightly apart from your other fingers. This provides the trigger finger effect as if you were holding a pistol. As you shake hands, your racket should be lying across your palm and fingers with your thumb and index finger forming a "V" on top of your racket handle. It is almost identical to the Eastern forehand grip in tennis. Check your partner's grip and ask her or him to check yours.

Success Goal = 3 correct handshake grips with your racket ___

Success Check
- Hold racket perpendicular to floor, edge down ___
- Form "V" on top of racket handle ___
- Grasp the racket firmly ___

To Increase Difficulty
- Execute the pistol grip with your eyes closed. Have your partner or teacher check your grip for correct position.
- Change to the background grip by placing the thumb in a straight up position on the top, left-hand bevel of the racket handle.

2. Shuttle Bounce

Use your pistol grip and bounce the shuttle off the face of your racket up in the air. Bounce the bird vertically off both sides of the racket face. This teaches you to keep your eyes on the bird and helps you to get the feel of the bird contacting the racket face. Continue until you can successfully bounce the bird several times without missing.

Success Goal = 30 consecutive bounces with your palm up ___
30 consecutive bounces with your palm down ___

Success Check
• Bump the bird into the air with your strings ___
• Lift your racket and allow the bird to travel only 1 to 2 feet (about half a meter) in the air ___

To Increase Difficulty
• Alternate hitting the shuttle with palm up and then palm down.
• Bump the bird 3 to 4 feet (about 1 meter) in the air.

3. Shuttle Scoop

Use the handshake grip with your palm up. Pick up or scoop up a bird lying on the floor, attempting to keep the bird on the racket face. Place your racket face next to the bird with the racket face held nearly parallel to the floor. Slide the racket quickly under the bird with a scooping action allowing the wrist to roll under, catching the bird on the racket face. This is usually done from the right side of the bird for right handers.

**Success Goal** = 3 successful attempts of scooping up bird without dropping it ___

Success Check
• Bird remains on racket face ___

To Increase Difficulty
• Scoop up the shuttle and toss it into the air, catching it with your opposite hand.
• Scoop up the shuttle, holding the racket palm down or with a backhand grip.
• Scoop up the shuttle from both the right side and the left side.

To Decrease Difficulty
• Place the shuttle on the floor pointing directly upward, feathers down. With the bird sitting up, it will more easily fall onto the racket face.

4. Ready Position

Assume the ready position, keeping your feet shoulder width apart with your knees slightly bent and your weight on the balls of your feet. Check your partner's stance and ask her or him to check yours.

Success Goal = 3 successful attempts of demonstrating the ready position ___

Success Check
- Hold racket head up, slightly on your backhand side ___
- Hold your nondominant arm up and slightly bent ___
- Keep your feet about shoulder width apart with your weight on the balls of your feet ___

5. Bird Carry

From the ready position, use the pistol grip with your palm up. Place a bird on your racket strings and walk to the net from the back boundary line using a step-close-step shuffle movement with your feet. Lead with your dominant foot, keeping the shuttle on the racket. Hold your nondominant arm up for balance.

Success Goal = 1 round trip to the net from the back boundary line ___

Success Check
- Handshake or pistol grip ___
- Palm up ___
- Lead with dominant foot ___

To Increase Difficulty
- Shuffle or skip to the net from the back boundary line as fast as possible without letting the bird fall off your racket face.
- With the bird on your strings, compete with your partner in a race from the back boundary line to the net and back.
- Use the pistol grip, holding your hand palm down or backhand. Place the bird on the strings and shuffle to and from the net.

To Decrease Difficulty
- Go slower and walk from the back boundary line to the net and back.

6. Footwork and Movement

Starting from center court and the ready position, touch the four corners of the court in succession, returning to the center position after each touch. Pivot and reach with your dominant arm and leg, and shuffle using a step-close-stepping action with your feet. Cross over only on your backhand side, not your forehand side.

Success Goal = touch the 4 corners of the court 20 times within 30 seconds, returning to midcourt following each corner touch ___

Success Check
• Reach with dominant hand ___
• Lead with dominant foot ___

To Increase Difficulty

• Perform the maximum number of touches that you can in 30 seconds.
• Simulate swinging at and hitting an imaginary bird at the end of each touch or reach.
• Without a racket in your hand, reach and touch the floor with your dominant hand.
• Use a sashay step instead of the normal step-close-step shuffle.
• Pivot, step-close-jump, and simulate a stroking action at the end. Return to center court. This jumping action requires much more energy, and you should attempt to stay under control and on balance, especially landing from the jump.

To Decrease Difficulty

• Slow down. Walk or shuffle your feet more slowly.

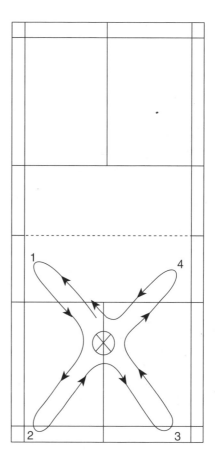

7. Speed Attack Drill

Player A is a setter who sends up a shot anywhere on the opposite side of the net to Player B. Player B responds and then charges the net. Player C is stationed near the net and tosses a short bird just over the net. Player B closes toward the net and tries to put the bird away. Player A should hit another shot as soon as Player B puts the bird away at the net. The drill is continuous for 30 seconds to 1 minute.

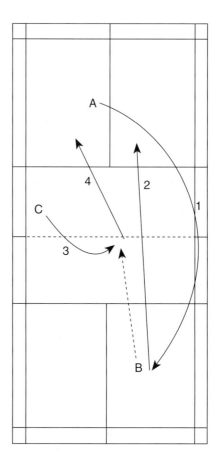

Success Goal = 30 to 60 seconds continuous drill without missing ___
sustain the drill for 6 consecutive returns without missing ___

✔ Success Check

• Use correct footwork in moving to the net ___
• Keep racket up as you near the net ___

To Increase Difficulty

• Increase the pace to make it more difficult for Player B to recover in time to smash again.
• Vary the height of the toss at the net so Player B has to hit a drive from the net instead of a smash.
• Have Player B leap in toward the net as soon as he thinks he can make contact.

To Decrease Difficulty

• Slow the pace to give Player B more time.
• Toss the bird at the net slightly higher to give Player B more time to get there.

8. Deep Base Attack Drill

Player A stands near the back boundary line and sends an underhand shot toward the opposite side of the net to Player B. Player B straddles his back doubles' service line and then charges the net as soon as the shot has been hit. Player B closes toward the net and tries to hit the bird high enough to allow him time to get back again. Player A should hit another shot as soon as Player B recovers to his backcourt. The drill is continuous for 30 seconds to 1 minute.

Success Goal = 60 seconds of continuous play without missing ___
sustain the drill for 6 consecutive returns without missing ___

Success Check
• Use correct footwork in moving to the net ___
• Keep racket up as you move and recover ___

To Increase Difficulty
• Increase the pace so Player B has less time to recover to get to the net again.
• Vary the direction of the shot so Player B has less time to recover from the net. Player A may increase the difficulty for Player B by sending shots to the right or left, perhaps with a fake.

To Decrease Difficulty
• Slow the pace to give Player B more time.
• Hit the bird at the net slightly higher to give Player B more time.

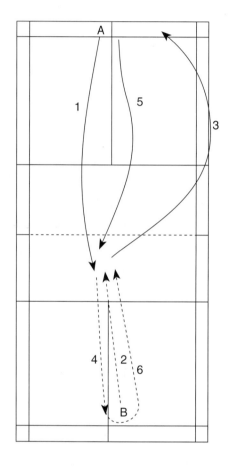

9. Footwork on Command

Player A gives verbal commands and hand gestures to direct Player B's movement around the badminton court. Player A does this with a preparatory command and a command of execution. The preparatory command identifies the general direction to be moved, such as back, front, or side. The command of execution tells the player whether the movement is to the forehand or backhand. A sequence of movement in 12 directions is recommended as follows:

1. Back forehand
2. Front forehand
3. Back backhand
4. Front backhand
5. Front forehand
6. Side backhand
7. Front backhand
8. Side forehand

Plus, you can choose four other commands at random. You can use hand gestures pointing in the appropriate direction of movement. As movement is accomplished to a given area of the court, Player B should also simulate a swing at an imaginary bird. After completing the simulated hit, recover to centercourt position as quickly as possible. Player A must allow a pause between commands long enough for Player B to sufficiently recover to midcourt.

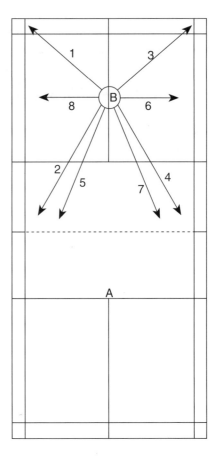

Success Goal = repeat the drill 3 times in succession ___

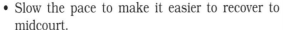

Success Check
• Use correct footwork in moving on the court ___
• Keep racket up as you move and recover ___

To Increase Difficulty
• Increase the pace to make it more difficult to re-cover in time to get to midcourt again.
• Vary the direction so Player B must wait and make sure of the appropriate direction before moving.

To Decrease Difficulty
• Slow the pace to make it easier to recover to midcourt.

RACKET HANDLING AND FOOTWORK SUCCESS SUMMARY

If you can handle your racket without thinking about it, assume your ready position, and readily move around your side of the court, you are on your way to becoming a better badminton player. In badminton, the lighter racket makes it possible for you to use wrist action initiated by forearm rotation to manipulate the racket at a great speed. The lighter object (shuttle) also makes possible greater use of your wrist without loss of control. This indicates that you need a firm grip at the instant you make contact. The handshake or pistol grip in badminton provides flexible and effortless movement of your wrist when hitting the bird.

Movement on the badminton court is concerned with reaching the shuttle in as few steps as possible while maintaining good balance and keeping your body under control. With practice, proper footwork eventually becomes habit and virtually an automatic aspect of your game.

Before you advance to the next step, ask a partner or teacher to rate your racket-handling skills and ready position using the "Keys to Success" checklists in Figures 1.2 and 1.3. Successful players enjoy playing and practicing every time they have an opportunity.

STEP

2 SERVES: LONG, SHORT, AND IN BETWEEN

T hink of serving in badminton as similar to being a waiter or waitress in a restaurant. A good waiter will provide good service and then receive good tips. In badminton, good serves give you a better opportunity to score points and win games.

In order to be a legal serve, contact with the shuttle must be made below your waist and the racket shaft must point downward. Your entire racket head must be discernibly below any part of your racket hand before striking the shuttle.

Why Is the Serve Important?

Your underhand serve puts the shuttle in play at the beginning of each rally and therefore, is probably your most important single stroke. It is difficult to score consistently without an adequate serve. Also, this stroke is often used to set up your partner for practicing strokes or for drills.

Your long serve is your basic singles' serve. This serve directs the shuttle high and deep, and the shuttle should turn over and fall as close to the back boundary line as possible. Thus the shuttle is more difficult to time and hit solidly, making all your opponent's returns less effective. The short, low serve is most often used in doubles' play. Because your doubles' service court is 30 inches (0.76 meters) shorter and 18 inches (0.46 meters) wider than your singles' service court, the low serve seems to be more effective in doubles. This serve may be delivered from

either the forehand or the backhand sides. Other in-between variations are the drive and the flick serves. These are good alternatives that give your opponent less time and may result in quick points. However, both are hit upward, and you should use them when they are least expected. Discussion later in this step and in Steps 9 and 10 address strategy for returning these serves effectively.

How to Execute the Long Serve

The long serve closely resembles a forehand underhand swinging motion. You should stand near the centerline and approximately 4 to 5 feet (1.5 meters) behind the short service line. This positions you close to center court and approximately equidistant from all of the corners. Your feet should be staggered up and back with your dominant foot back (see Figure 2.1a). Your forefinger and thumb of your nondominant hand should hold the shuttle at its base, extended in front of your body about waist level. Hold your racket arm in a backswing position with your hand and wrist in a cocked position. As you release the shuttle, transfer your weight from your back foot to your forward foot and pull your arm down to contact the shuttle at approximately knee height (see Figure 2.1b). Your forearm rotation and wrist action provide most of the power. Your follow-through is up in line with the path of the shuttle and finishes over your opposite shoulder (see Figure 2.1c).

FIGURE 2.1 **KEYS TO SUCCESS**

LONG SERVE

a   b   c

Preparation

1. Handshake or pistol grip ___
2. Up and back stance ___
3. Hold bird at waist level ___
4. Put weight on rear foot ___
5. Racket arm in backswing ___
6. Cock wrist ___

Execution

1. Shift weight ___
2. Use forearm pronation and wrist action ___
3. Contact at knee level ___
4. High and deep ___

Follow-Through

1. Finish with racket upward and in line with the bird's flight ___
2. Cross racket in front of and over opposite shoulder ___
3. Roll hips and shoulders around ___

How to Execute the Short Serve

Make your short serve with the same preparation as your long serve. The primary exception is that you should stand much closer to the short service line, perhaps within 6 inches (15 centimeters) or less. Your racket arm begins in a similar backswing position, with your hand and wrist in a cocked position (see Figure 2.2a). As you release the shuttle, transfer your weight from your back foot to your forward foot and pull your arm down to contact the shuttle below waist height. However, as your racket hand comes forward, there is little or no wrist action because the shuttle

is guided or pushed over the net rather than hit (see Figure 2.2b). The follow-through is short with your racket finishing up and in line with the serve (see Figure 2.2c).

Contact your backhand short serve in front of your body with a square or slightly staggered stance (see Figure 2.3b; page 25). This backhand serve has several advantages: (1) it travels a shorter distance; (2) it gets across the net and to your opponent sooner; and (3) it tends to blend in with your clothing and provides a form of camouflage. Some players actually stand on their tiptoes to serve a higher and slightly flatter trajectory.

FIGURE
2.2 **KEYS TO SUCCESS**

FOREHAND SHORT SERVE

a   b   c

Preparation

1. Handshake or pistol grip ___
2. Up and back stance ___
3. Hold bird at waist level ___
4. Put weight on rear foot ___
5. Racket arm in backswing postion ___
6. Cock wrist ___

Execution

1. Shift weight back to front ___
2. Use little or no wrist action ___
3. Contact at thigh level ___
4. Push or guide shuttle ___
5. Low, close to net ___

Follow-Through

1. Finish with racket upward in line with the bird's flight ___
2. Cross racket over in front of opposite shoulder ___
3. Roll hips and shoulders around ___

How to Execute the Drive and Flick Serves

If your low serve is temporarily inconsistent or if your opponents are anticipating your short serve, you may use the drive and flick serves to keep your opponents honest. The drive is a low, flat serve usually directed to your opponent's backhand. The advantages of this driven serve are its quickness and unexpectedness. Hold your racket arm in a backswing position with your hand and wrist in a cocked position (see Figure 2.4; page 26). As you release the shuttle, transfer your weight from your back foot to your forward foot and pull your arm down to contact the shuttle below waist height. However, as your racket hand comes forward, snap your racket through with vigorous fore-

arm rotation and wrist action. The follow-through is longer than the short serve with your racket finishing up and in line with the serve.

The flick should also resemble the short serve, but is delivered by quickly uncocking your wrist (see Figure 2.4). Your racket arm begins in a similar backswing, cocked position. As you release the shuttle, transfer your weight from your back foot to your forward foot and pull your arm down to contact the shuttle below waist height. However, as your racket hand comes forward, there is vigorous wrist action as the shuttle is hit higher than your opponent can reach, but not high enough for him or her to get back and make an effective return. The follow-through is longer, similar to the drive serve. You may also effectively deliver both the drive and flick serves from your backhand side.

FIGURE
2.3

KEYS TO SUCCESS

BACKHAND SHORT SERVE

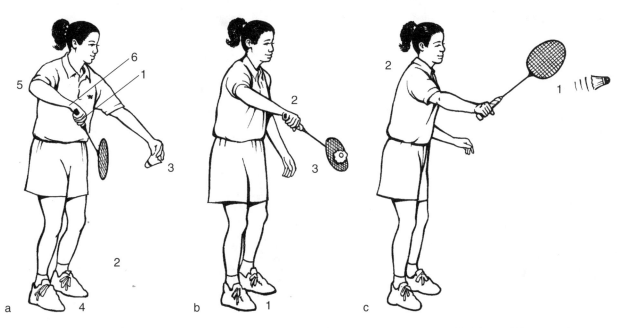

a b c

Preparation

1. Handshake or pistol grip ___
2. Square stance ___
3. Hold bird at waist level ___
4. Put weight on both feet ___
5. Racket arm in backswing ___
6. Cock wrist ___

Execution

1. Put weight on balls of feet or up on toes ___
2. Use little or no wrist action ___
3. Contact at thigh level ___
4. Push or guide shuttle ___
5. Low, close to net ___

Follow-Through

1. Finish with racket upward in line with the bird's flight ___
2. Cross racket over in front of same shoulder ___
3. Roll hips and shoulders around and finish with both arms up ___

How to Return Serves

Your return of serve is important because it determines your opponent's success in scoring points. A good return allows little chance for scoring opportunities. Each return should allow much room for error and yet pressure your opponent to force a weak return.

Your return of serve should open up the court and reduce the possible angle of return by your opponent. It should also give you as much time as possible and very little time for your opponent. Singles' returns of serve should have the possibility of being directed to all four corners of the court. They should make your opponent move the greatest distance possible. Doubles' returns of serve should be pushed and misdirected. Every return should be hit downward if possible. Every return should attempt to force an upward return by your opponent.

FIGURE 2.4

KEYS TO SUCCESS

DRIVE AND FLICK SERVES

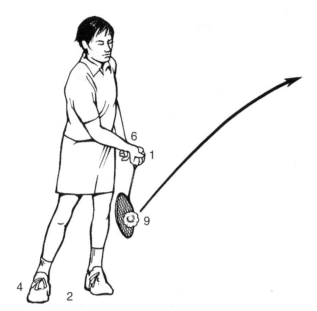

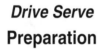

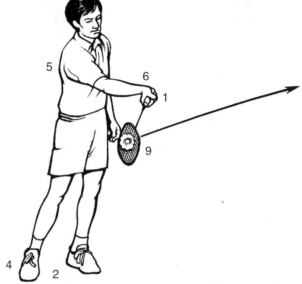

Drive Serve
Preparation

1. Handshake or pistol grip ___
2. Up and back stance ___
3. Hold bird at waist level ___
4. Put weight on rear foot ___
5. Racket arm in backswing ___
6. Cock wrist ___

Execution

7. Shift weight ___
8. Use vigorous wrist action and forearm rotation ___
9. Contact at thigh level ___
10. Quick, low, flat shot ___

Follow-Through

11. Finish with racket upward in line with the bird's flight ___
12. Finish swing quickly to recover in ready position ___
13. Both arms finish up, prepared for quick return ___

Flick Serve
Preparation

1. Handshake or pistol grip ___
2. Up and back stance ___
3. Hold bird at waist level ___
4. Put weight on rear foot ___
5. Racket arm in backswing ___
6. Cock wrist ___

Execution

7. Shift weight ___
8. Use vigorous wrist action and forearm rotation ___
9. Contact at thigh level ___
10. Looped higher, out of reach ___

Follow-Through

11. Finish with racket upward in line with the bird's flight ___
12. Finish swing quickly to recover in ready position ___
13. Both arms finish up, prepared for quick return ___

SERVE SUCCESS STOPPERS

Lack of practice usually causes problems with consistency and placement of your serve and service return. Few players concentrate enough on their serve and return of serve. You should spend additional practice time to develop an accurate and effective serve and service return for both singles and doubles.

Error	Correction
1. You often serve the bird into the net.	1. Angle the racket face slightly more open to direct serve higher.
2. You consistently serve the bird too high over the net on short serve.	2. Close the face of your racket to hit a flatter trajectory.
3. You consistently serve the bird long, out of the singles' court.	3. Move your starting position farther back so it's nearer the center of the court.
4. Your receiver seems to be able to rush and put away your serve.	4. Mix up your serves, both in their types and in their direction or placement.
5. Your receiver stands very close, almost on her short service line.	5. Serve a mixture of high and wide serves to get her off the short service line.
6. You feel intimidated and self-conscious before your serve.	6. Focus on the bird as long as possible. Try to see the bird hit your racket, and don't watch your opponent's body movements before serving.
7. You experience an inconsistent serve, fatigue, or lack of confidence.	7. Try to be in good shape and concentrate. Fatigue often causes inconsistency. Mental and physical practice will give you consistency and confidence.
8. You swing and miss the shuttle altogether on serve.	8. Suspend a bird from a string and hold it at knee level. Hold the string securely or hang it from a net and take several practice swings. You may also shorten your swing, shorten your grip on the handle, or drop the bird from a lower height.
9. You return long serve too short or near midcourt.	9. Direct your return of the long serve to the four corners of your opponent's court.
10. You make a clear return of short serve or hit it up to opponents.	10. Push or misdirect your return down either sideline past the opponent nearest the net.

SERVE

DRILLS

1. Long Serve

Start with the handshake or pistol grip. Stand close to the centerline and behind the short service line on your court. Serve 30 forehand long serves from each side. A good serve should land in the court diagonally opposite your service court and just past the doubles' back service line or in the back alley. Adjust your starting position accordingly, but attempt to serve from as close to your center court as comfortably possible. If you are hitting your serves past the back boundary line, move your starting position farther back from the short service line. If you are hitting your serves consistently short, try to emphasize rolling your hips and shoulders into the long serve. Exaggerate the height if necessary to get the shuttle to turn over and fall in a perpendicular path as close to the back boundary line as possible.

Success Goal = 30 good long serves per practice session ___

Success Check
• Stagger your feet up and back ___
• Roll hips and shoulders into serve, rotating your forearm and wrist vigorously ___
• Drive your long serve up, high, and deep ___

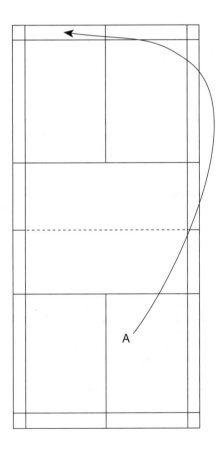

To Increase Difficulty
• Use a heavier racket, such as a tennis racket, for more resistance.
• Overload or increase your resistance by using a racket chute or racket cover.
• Use a shuttle that is specifically designed to be slower (green band, blue band, etc.).

To Decrease Difficulty
• Serve from closer to the net on your side.
• Use a much lighter racket to develop more racket speed and hit the shuttle faster.
• Use a shuttle that is faster (red band, etc.) by design, such as an outdoor bird.
• Drop and hit the long serve into a high, flat wall until you are consistently making good contact with the shuttle.
• Another alternative is to suspend a shuttle with a string from a goal or the net at your knee level. Practice your underhand long serve until you can consistently make good contact with the shuttle.

2. Short Serve Drill

Start with the handshake or pistol grip. Stand close to the centerline and close behind the short service line on your court. Serve 30 forehand short serves from each side. A good serve should land in the court diagonally opposite your service court and just past the short service line. Position yourself as close to your short service line as possible. If you are hitting your serves into the net, move your starting position farther back from the short service line. If you are hitting your serves consistently short, try to emphasize hitting the shuttle more in front of you in order to shorten the distance to your opponent's court. Push, guide, or direct the shuttle into the "T" area, which is the shortest distance. Repeat the 30 serves from each side using the backhand short serve. When using the backhand short serve, rise on your tiptoes to serve from a higher position. This will allow you to serve the shuttle flatter and still clear the net on your short serve.

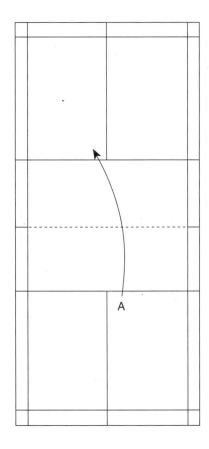

Success Goal = 30 good forehand short serves ___
30 good backhand short serves ___

Success Check

- Stagger your feet up and back for forehand; square feet for backhand ___
- Drop shuttle from approximately waist high for forehand; from in front of racket for backhand ___
- Contact serve about thigh high for forehand; hip high for backhand ___

To Increase Difficulty

- Alternate short serves from near the centerline to out wide to alley.
- Attempt to serve backhand short serves with your eyes closed. Feel the serve.

To Decrease Difficulty

- Serve from closer to the net on your side.
- Bend the elbow on your racket arm to shorten the lever and get the shuttle closer to you.
- If your serves are falling short, use a shuttle that is faster (red band, etc.) by design, such as an outdoor bird.
- If your serves are too high or long, use a shuttle that is specifically designed to be slower (green band, blue band, etc.).

A

3. Drive and Flick Serve Drill

Start with the handshake or pistol grip. Stand close to the centerline and close behind the short service line on your court. Serve 30 forehand drive serves and flick serves from each side. A good drive serve should be a low, flat, driven serve that lands in your opponent's backhand side of their service court. A good flick serve should be a looped, deep serve that lands in your opponent's backhand side of their service court. Adjust your starting position accordingly, but attempt to serve from as close to your short service line as comfortably possible. If you are hitting your serves into the net, move your starting position farther back from the short service line. If you are hitting your serves consistently short, try to emphasize snapping your racket through the shuttle with a quick uncocking of the wrist. Exaggerate the height on the drive serve if necessary to get the shuttle over your opponent's reach and as close to the back boundary line as possible. Repeat drill using the backhand.

Success Goal = 30 good forehand drive serves ___
30 good backhand drive serves ___
30 good forehand flick serves ___
30 good backhand flick serves ___

Success Check
• Underhand hit ___
• Drop shuttle from approximately waist high ___
• Snap your racket through using vigorous forearm rotation and wrist action into serve ___
• Contact serve about thigh high ___
• Drive is a quick, low, flat shot; flick is looped just beyond opponent's reach ___

To Increase Difficulty
• Alternate serves deep near the centerline to deep, out wide to alley.
• Alternate forehand serves with backhand serves.
• Alternate drive and flick serves.

To Decrease Difficulty
• Serve farther away from the net on your side.
• Use a shuttle that is faster (red band, etc.) by design, such as an outdoor bird.

Flick

Drive

4. Four Corners Target Drill

Player A serves high to Player B who is receiving in his right service court. Player B attempts to hit a shot to one of the four corners of the singles' court. A target, such as a towel or racket cover, may be placed in each corner. Points may be kept for each target hit. After a total of 10 targets has been hit, players may switch roles. Or after 10 attempts, Player B may want to assess how accurately he directed the bird to the four corners of the court by noting visually where the shots landed.

 **Success Goal** = 10 targets hit ___

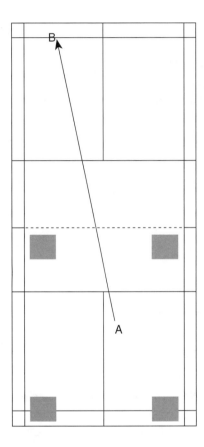

Success Check

• Assess how accurately you directed the bird to the four corners of the court by noting visually where your shots landed ___

5. Target Serve Drill

Place a large cardboard box in your opponent's service court. Look at the target before you deliver the serve. Push or guide the short serve just past the short service line. Lift the high, deep serve so the bird turns over and falls perpendicular to the back boundary line. Drive and flick serves may also be directed toward targets in your opponent's service court.

 **Success Goal** = 5 out of 10 hits into box ___

Success Check
• Begin with your feet up and back ___
• Shift your weight forward as you swing ___
• Contact your serve below your waist ___

 To Increase Difficulty
• Place the targets in specific areas of the service court (for example, at the "T").
• Set up smaller targets (for example, a towel, a racket cover, or a smaller box).

To Decrease Difficulty
• Set up larger targets.
• Move targets to various corners of the service court.

6. Under the Rope Drill

Attach a rope or cord approximately 18 inches (half a meter) above and parallel to the top of the net. Push or guide your short serves under the rope and into the appropriate service court. Serve most of your short serves to the "T" (the intersection of the short service line and the centerline). This is the shortest distance, so the bird will get to your opponent sooner and thus give him or her less time to return it. Doing this will also give your opponent less of an angle for returns.

Success Goal = 6 out of 10 serves under the rope and in the proper court ___

Success Check
• Begin with your feet up and back, near the short service line ___
• Shift your weight forward as you swing ___
• Contact your serve below your waist ___

 To Increase Difficulty
• Place the targets in specific areas of the service court (for example, on the outside corners).
• Lower the rope to make the serving area smaller.

To Decrease Difficulty
• Raise the rope to make the serving area larger.
• Serve from farther back from the net.

7. Over the Rope Drill

Tie a rope or cord about 10 feet (3 meters) high above the middle of your opponent's service court. Lift your long serves over the rope and into the proper service court. Serve most of your long serves into the back alley of your opponent's singles' service court. The shuttle will drop almost perpendicular to the floor, which requires your opponent to move to his or her backcourt to return the serve.

Success Goal = 6 out of 10 serves over the rope and in the proper court ___

Success Check
- Begin with your feet up and back, approximately 3 feet (1 meter) behind the short service line ___
- Shift your weight forward as you swing ___
- Lift the bird high and deep ___

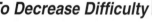

To Increase Difficulty
- Place targets in the corners of the back alley of the singles' service court.
- Raise the rope higher.
- Move farther back from the net.

To Decrease Difficulty
- Lower the rope.
- Move closer to the net.

SERVE SUCCESS SUMMARY

If you can serve a variety of serves and readily mix up your service selection during a game or match, you are on your way to becoming a better badminton player. The ability to incorporate numerous different serves puts more pressure on your opponent and improves your chances of succeeding in badminton. The long, short, drive, and flick serves all provide a different look for your opponent and force her to play you more honestly when she receives your serve. Varying your serves makes them more difficult for your opponent to anticipate, and therefore increases your potential for scoring points on your serve.

Before you advance to the next step, ask a partner or coach to rate your success at serving using the "Keys to Success" checklists (see Figures 2.1-2.4). Play and practice your various serves at every opportunity.

STEP 3
OVERHEAD STROKES: FOREHAND AND BACKHAND

The overhead is the most important tactical stroke in badminton play. Think of the overhead stroke as a tactical nuclear weapon with multiple warheads. All the four basic shots in badminton may be delivered from the forehand or backhand sides and with an overhand action: the clear, the smash, the drop shot, and the drive. You can use both forehand and backhand to move your opponent around the court.

The forehand is played with a full, throwing motion from the back half of your court. The backhand is played with a full, upward extension of your dominant arm from the backhand corner of your court and is a mirror image of the forehand stroke. If you showed a film of your forehand overhead in reverse, you would see a replica of your backhand. The extension of your arm at the elbow and vigorous forearm rotation provide most of the power for your overhead strokes. Forearm pronation occurs on your forehand stroke, and forearm supination occurs on your backhand stroke. Anatomically, your forearm works or rotates only in these two ways. Classical wrist flexion or "wrist snap" occurs very little, if at all. The proper technique allows your wrist to uncock naturally, with the racket following through in the direction of your return.

Why Is the Forehand Overhead Stroke Important?

The forehand overhead stroke is probably the most powerful aspect of a player's game. You may employ it as an offensive or a defensive shot to move your opponent into his backcourt, up to the net, or to the side. A good overhead stroke from backcourt should attempt to make all the shots look the same. Then your opponent cannot determine which shot you are playing until after you have contacted the shuttle. If you disguise your shots well enough, the shuttle may not be returned at all. The difference between the various shots lies in the point of contact between the shuttle and your racket. Thus, the angle at which the shuttle leaves the racket and the speed of your racket at contact determine the speed of the returning shuttle.

How to Execute the Forehand Overhead Stroke

The handshake grip is used when hitting shots on your dominant side, which in most cases is your right side (see Figure 3.1a). The forehand overhead stroking motion is similar to throwing a ball. The mechanics are almost identical. A good performance of this throwing motion is defined as the properly timed coordination of accelerations and decelerations of all body segments that produces maximum absolute velocity to your dominant hand and in turn to your racket.

The overhead strokes will usually be made from the back half of your court. As the shuttle is hit upward to your end of the court, turn your body so your feet are perpendicular to the net. Point your nondominant shoulder toward the net and shift your weight to your rear foot. If necessary, skip backward until you are slightly behind the dropping shuttle. This is your hitting stance.

As you move to the oncoming shuttle, raise your racket arm, cock your wrist, and point your racket slightly upward as your shoulders turn into your hitting position (see Figure 3.1b). When you make your stroke, several things occur very rapidly. Your forward swing begins with a drive off your rear leg, followed by hip and shoulder rotation. Extend your nonracket arm in front of your body for balance and assistance in rotating your upper body. The racket head drops down behind your head into a backscratch position. Your dominant arm extends upward led by your elbow and vigorous rotation of your forearm and wrist. Throw your racket up to meet the shuttle with the edge of the racket leading. However, the rapid pronation of your forearm causes the racket face to rotate until it is almost flat at contact. The angle of the racket face determines the direction of the shuttle. At contact, the rapid rotation of your forearm has provided most of the power, with your wrist

uncocking so your arm is fully extended. Contact the shuttle at the highest possible point and in front of the body.

Your hand and wrist allow the racket to follow through naturally, pronating and finishing downward with your racket hand rolling over, palm facing the outside. There is little or no wrist flexion or wrist snap. Your racket travels through the contact area and then downward in line with the flight of the shuttle (see Figure 3.1c). Your racket then crosses in front of and on the opposite side of your body. Your rear foot swings forward in a scissors action continuing your weight transfer and possibly providing momentum for additional height and power.

FIGURE 3.1 — **KEYS TO SUCCESS**

FOREHAND OVERHEAD STROKE

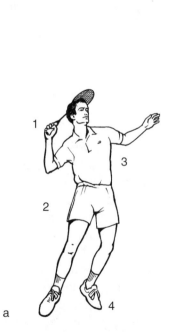

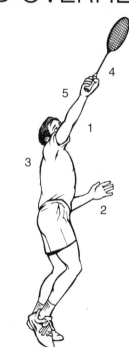

Preparation

1. Handshake or pistol grip ___
2. Sideways hitting stance ___
3. Both arms up ___
4. Put weight on rear foot ___

Execution

1. Elbow leads arm extension ___
2. Move nondominant arm down ___
3. Rotate upper body ___
4. Reach high to hit ___
5. Pronate forearm ___

Follow-Through

1. Racket hand finishes palm out ___
2. Racket finishes down in line with bird's flight ___
3. Cross racket to opposite side of your body ___
4. Swing rear foot forward with scissors action ___
5. Continue weight transfer ___

Why Is the Backhand Overhead Stroke Important?

The backhand overhead stroke allows you to return your opponent's shots from your backhand side even when they are completely behind you. With the proper footwork and stroking technique, your backhand saves you time and energy and can produce effective offensive or defensive shots. A good backhand overhead stroke should attempt to make all of your shots look the same. Then the opponent cannot determine which shot you are playing until after you have contacted the shuttle. If you disguise your shots well enough, the shuttle may not be returned at all. As on the forehand, the difference between the various shots lies in the point of contact between the shuttle and your racket. Thus, the angle at which the shuttle leaves the racket and the speed of your racket at contact determine the speed of the returning shuttle.

How to Execute the Backhand Overhead Stroke

The backhand overhead motion can be compared to popping a towel at the ceiling. A good performance of this backhand throwing motion produces rapid extension of your dominant arm and maximum velocity to your racket head and in turn to the shuttle. These strokes will usually be made from the rear one-third of your court. As the shuttle is hit upward to your backhand, pivot and turn your body so your back is toward the net. Reach or lead with your dominant foot toward the backhand corner. Shift your weight to that rear foot. If necessary, step-close or shuffle backward until you are slightly behind the dropping shuttle. This is your hitting stance.

The backhand version of the handshake grip places your thumb straight up and down on the left-hand, top bevel of the handle, instead of wrapped around it (see Figure 3.2a). This thumb-up grip enables you to hit returns from your nondominant side without changing your grip. It also provides added support and leverage for all your backhand strokes. This is primarily a finger pressure change made by merely loosening your hold on the racket and then assuming the new hold.

When you do have more time, such as on a high, deep clear to the backhand, a slight turn to the left from the recommended backhand grip provides more power. This places the knuckle of your forefinger on the top plate of the handle and your thumb diagonally across and up the back of the handle. However, this grip resembles the Eastern backhand grip in tennis and effectively locks your wrist. As long as you contact the shuttle in front of your body, this presents no problem. But in badminton play, the shuttle is often hit deep to your backhand corner and you must hit the shuttle when it is past you or behind you. When this happens, the Eastern backhand grip becomes a liability. The previously recommended backhand grip, which is similar to the forehand grip, allows greater wrist action. It permits the face of your racket to direct the shuttle into your opponent's court even when your back is to the net and the shuttle is significantly behind or to the side of you.

As you move to the oncoming shuttle, raise your racket arm, cock your wrist, and point your racket slightly upward as your shoulders turn into the hitting position. When you make the stroke, several things occur very rapidly (see Figure 3.2b). The upward swing begins with a drive off your rear leg, followed by hip and shoulder rotation. Lift your arm from the shoulder with the forearm parallel to the floor and the racket head pointed downward. Extend your dominant arm upward, led by your elbow, and vigorously rotate your forearm and wrist. Throw up your racket to meet the shuttle with the racket edge leading. However, the rapid supination of the forearm causes the racket face to rotate until it is almost flat at contact. The racket face angle determines the direction of the bird. At contact, the rapid rotation of your forearm has provided most of the power, with your wrist uncocking so your arm is fully extended. Contact the shuttle at the highest possible point and preferably in front of your body. Your hand and wrist allow your racket to follow through naturally, supinating your forearm and finishing downward (see Figure 3.2c). There is little or no wrist flexion or wrist snap. Your racket travels through the contact area and then downward in line with your return. Your rear foot pushes forward and helps you rotate around to again face the net and propel you back toward the center of your court. This weight transfer may also provide added momentum and power for your shot.

FIGURE 3.2   KEYS TO SUCCESS

BACKHAND OVERHEAD STROKE

a   b   c

Preparation	**Execution**	**Follow-Through**

Preparation

1. Handshake or pistol grip with thumb on top, left-hand bevel ___
2. Sideways to backward hitting stance ___
3. Hold racket arm up with forearm parallel to the floor, racket head pointed down ___
4. Put weight on rear, dominant foot ___

Execution

1. Elbow leads arm extension ___
2. Move nondominant arm down ___
3. Rotate upper body ___
4. Reach high to hit ___
5. Supinate forearm ___
6. Racket head follows through ___

Follow-Through

1. Racket follow-through contact area downward in line with the return ___
2. Push forward with rear foot to propel you back toward center court ___
3. Use weight transfer to provide added momentum and power ___

OVERHEAD STROKE SUCCESS STOPPERS

Errors or idiosyncrasies are apparent at all levels of badminton competition. Even world-class competitors often demonstrate poor technique and improper stroke production. Correct stroke production is a result of proper practice and will provide more success on the court.

Error	Correction
1. Your overhead lacks power.	1. Increase your racket speed at the top of your swing. Shift your weight forward as you swing. Use the correct grip and attempt to develop more forearm pronation and supination.
2. You lack arm extension.	2. Many beginners fail to extend their arms completely when throwing the racket upward to hit an overhead stroke. Throw your racket upward as if attempting to scrape the ceiling. Do not "short arm" your forehand or backhand overhead stroke.
3. Your contact point is inconsistent.	3. Another common problem is failing to contact the shuttle over your racket shoulder. Instead, the shuttle is hit off to your side or behind your body. Move quickly to get behind the oncoming shuttle and keep your racket up. This problem is generally corrected by concentrating and hustling to get into position.
4. You have no deception.	4. A lack of deception is usually a result of failing to get your upper body turned on the backswing for every shot. Beginners often telegraph their drop shots by using the Western or frying pan grip and by hitting with their body square to the net. Turn sideways and (a) point your nondominant shoulder toward the net before your forehand, and (b) point your dominant shoulder toward the net before your backhand.
5. You have an incorrect backhand grip.	5. Use the handshake grip. The thumb-up grip on the backhand side allows you to hit shots that are behind you.

OVERHEAD STROKE

DRILLS
1. Racket Cover Overload Drill

Practice your full forehand and backhand swings throwing motion with the racket cover on your racket. The added weight and air resistance aid in developing strength and endurance in your hitting arm. Lead with your elbow.

Success Goal = 30 forehand swings ___
30 backhand swings ___

**Success Check**
- Throw racket ___
- Extend arm ___
- Reach high ___

2. Mirror Drill

Practice your forehand or backhand overhead with a full swing throwing motion facing a mirror. The mirror will give you visual feedback. If this is not possible, practice swinging on the court. Emphasize reaching as high as possible and snapping your racket through the contact area. Make your racket swish.

Success Goal = 30 forehand swings ___
30 backhand swings ___

 **Success Check**
• Shift weight ___
• Reach high ___
• Swing fast ___

3. Backhand Towel Drill

Stand with your back to a high, flat wall. Grasp the end of a small towel in your dominant hand. Extend your dominant arm up with the back of your arm touching the wall. Snap or pop the towel upward, emphasizing a vigorous rotation of your dominant arm.

 **Success Goal** = 5 minutes per practice session ___

Success Check
• Flex dominant arm at elbow ___
• Snap or pop towel ___
• Reach high ___

4. Wall Rally Drill

Practice your forehand or backhand overhead strokes by rallying with yourself against a high, flat wall. Emphasize a high, deep return similar to the clear to have enough time to prepare before each hit. Lead with your elbow and drive the shuttle up, high, and deep. Turn and get your racket back.

 **Success Goal** = 5 minutes on the forehand ___
5 minutes on the backhand ___

 **Success Check**
• Hold racket back and up ___
• Shoulders rotate, elbow leads ___
• Hit high and deep ___

5. Overhead Toss to Yourself

Place a shuttle on your racket face, with your racket hand held palm up. Stand sideways near the backcourt. Toss the shuttle upward with a lifting motion, placing the shuttle overhead for either a forehand or a backhand overhead stroke. After the shuttle leaves your racket, quickly lift your arm from the shoulder, placing your racket head downward at the end of your backswing. Extend your racket arm upward, leading with the elbow. Vigorously rotate your forearm and wrist, propelling the racket up to meet the shuttle at the highest possible point of contact. Shift your weight from your back foot to your front foot. Your racket face should direct the shuttle up and out, with your hand leading the racket before contacting the shuttle. It is not a rally; therefore, you need to begin with five to six shuttles. This is a repetitive drill in which you should execute at least 30 good returns. Good returns need to land near or beyond the doubles' service line in backcourt.

Success Goal = 30 good forehand clears ___
30 good backhand clears ___

Success Check
- Point elbow upward with racket pointed downward ___
- Hand leads racket upward toward shuttle ___
- Swing fast ___

To Increase Difficulty
- Recover to the ready position following each attempt.
- Alternate hitting forehand and backhand shots.
- Move toward the net and touch the short service line after each attempt and then recover to backcourt.
- Use a tennis racket instead of your badminton racket. The increased weight provides more of an overload.

To Decrease Difficulty
- Have your body already turned in a sideways hitting stance.
- Begin with the racket already pointing upward.
- Begin with the weight already shifted to the front foot.

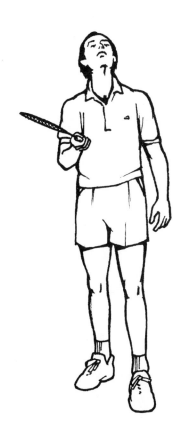

6. High Serve and Overhead Return

Player A serves a high, deep serve crosscourt to Player B. Player B clears straight ahead with a forehand overhead throwing action. Player E returns shuttles to Player A. Rotate positions after three attempts. Player A takes the place of Player E, B replaces A, and E moves behind Player D, and so on until all players have been at each position.

Success Goal = 3 good forehand clears from each position ___

Success Check
- Point elbow upward with racket pointed downward ___
- Elbow leads initial extension of arm ___
- Hand leads racket upward toward shuttle ___

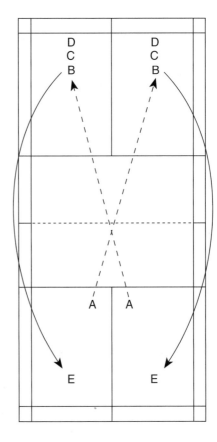

7. Chair Tag

Place a chair at the center of one side of the court. Player A stands on this side in her back forehand corner. Player B hits a high, deep serve to Player A's forehand corner. Player A clears straight ahead back to Player B and then attempts to run and touch the chair. She then returns to her forehand corner and the rally continues indefinitely.

 **Success Goal** = 3 good forehand clears from each position ___

 Success Check
• Elbow leads initial extension of arm ___
• Swing fast ___
• Place shot high and deep ___

To Increase Difficulty
• Player B may lower the height of her return to give Player A less time to recover.

To Decrease Difficulty
• Player B may raise the height of her return to give Player A more time to recover.

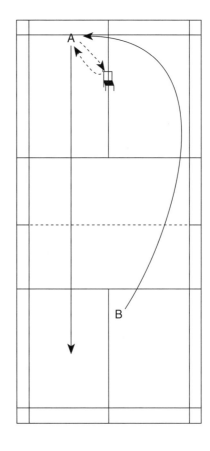

8. Shuttle Clears

Player A hits a high, underhand clear and runs to the opposite end of the court behind Player E. Sequence continues with each player clearing the shuttle from his forehand or backhand and running to the end of the line on the opposite end of the court.

Success Goal = 30 good forehand clears in succession ___
30 good backhand clears in succession ___

Success Check
• Point elbow upward with racket pointed downward ___
• Elbow leads initial extension of arm ___
• Hand leads racket upward toward shuttle ___

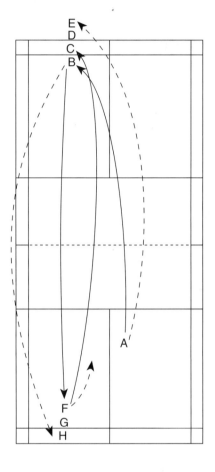

OVERHEAD STROKE SUCCESS SUMMARY

As you prepare to be observed and evaluated on your overhead, remember to turn sideways to the net and roll your hips and shoulders into your stroke. Your forehand overhead stroke should have a smooth transition from weight shift to vigorous upper body rotation, followed by arm extension and pronation, and finishing with your racket snapping through the shuttle at contact. Allow your hand and racket to follow through naturally. Complete the stroke by swinging your racket leg through in a scissors movement.

As you prepare to be observed and evaluated on your backhand overhead, remember to turn backward to the net and roll your hips and shoulders into the stroke. Your backhand overhead stroke should have a smooth transition from weight shift to vigorous upper body rotation. This is followed by arm extension and supination and finished with your racket snapping through the shuttle at contact. Allow your hand and racket to follow through naturally. Complete the stroke by pushing off and propelling yourself back toward midcourt.

Practice until your overhead is a continuous, rhythmic motion that results in an effective, accurate, and powerful stroke. When you feel that you are ready, ask someone to observe you and rate your performance using the "Keys to Success" checklists (see Figures 3.1-3.2). Try to visualize each overhead stroke and critique your thoughts out loud with your observer.

STEP 4

CLEAR: HIGH AND DEEP

The high, deep clear is usually used to gain time to return to the centercourt position. It is often recommended strategy, particularly in singles' play. When in doubt, clear! The defensive clear is a high return similar to the lob in tennis. The clear may be hit with an underhand or overhand stroke on either your forehand or backhand to force your opponent deep into her backcourt. It is also used in combination with the drop shot to run your opponent and make her defend all four corners of the court.

You should always try to hit the bird as soon as possible so your opponents will have less time to get to their shots. Take overhead and underhand returns at the highest possible contact point. As you move into position to hit the clear, throw your racket upward, meeting the shuttle with a flat racket with your elbow extending. Because the shuttle should go high and deep, swing your racket forward and up with your hand leading. Then your follow-through finishes in the direction of the bird's flight.

Why Is the Clear Important?

The primary value of the clear during competition is to keep the shuttle away from your opponent and make him or her move quickly. By getting the bird behind your opponents or making them move more rapidly than they would like, they will have less time and will become more fatigued. If you clear correctly, they will need to hurry to execute their returns accurately and effectively. The offensive clear is a flatter, faster clear, which is useful in getting the shuttle behind your opponents and potentially causing them to hit weak returns. The defensive clear has a high and deep trajectory.

How to Execute the Forehand Clear

When the shuttle is hit to you during a rally, you should move into a position behind the oncoming shuttle and assume your handshake grip. If you are returning with a forehand overhead clear, you should turn your shoulders and pivot at your waist to get sideways to the net. As the shuttle drops in the hitting area, swing your racket upward to contact the shuttle, directing it high and deep (see Figure 4.1). Contact the shuttle in front of your body and as high as possible with the racket finishing in the direction of the shuttle's trajectory. The defensive clear is directed upward, high over your opponent's head. The offensive clear follows a flatter, faster trajectory just out of your opponent's reach.

Your hand and wrist allow your racket arm to follow through naturally. Rapid forearm pronation provides most of the power. Your racket travels through the contact area and then forward in line with the flight of the shuttle. At or very soon after contact on the overhead or underhand clear, transfer your body weight rapidly as your feet push your body back toward midcourt.

If you are clearing from near the net, you should use an underhand stroke. Reach with the dominant arm and place the racket face under the dropping return. As the shuttle drops in the hitting area, swing your racket upward to contact the shuttle, directing it high and deep (see Figure 4.1). Contact the shuttle with your racket hand, palm up, in front of your body and as high as possible, directing the shuttle upward, high, and deep. Your racket finishes in the direction of the shuttle's trajectory.

FIGURE 4.1   **KEYS TO SUCCESS**

FOREHAND CLEAR

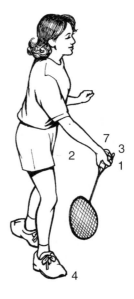

Overhead Clear
Preparation

1. Handshake or pistol grip ___
2. Recover into waiting or receiving stance ___
3. Hold racket arm up with racket head up ___
4. Distribute weight evenly on both feet ___

Execution

5. Reach with the dominant foot ___
6. Pivot and turn in the direction of shuttle ___
7. Wrist in laid back or cocked position ___
8. Forward swing to contact high as possible ___
9. Pronate forearm ___
10. Racket head follows through ___

Follow-Through

11. Continue swing up with shuttle's flight ___
12. Swing toward the net ___
13. Racket arm rotates ___
14. Push off back toward midcourt ___
15. Return to center court ___

Underhand Clear
Preparation

1. Forehand handshake, pistol grip ___
2. Reach with dominant hand and foot ___
3. Racket arm up with palm pointed upward ___
4. Put weight slightly on front foot ___

Execution

5. Pivot and reach for the oncoming shuttle ___
6. Place racket under dropping shuttle ___
7. Put wrist in laid back or cocked position ___
8. Drop racket down and swing it up ___
9. Contact shuttle as high as possible ___
10. Pronate your forearm ___

Follow-Through

11. Continue swing up with shuttle's flight ___
12. Rotate forearm ___
13. Push off with your feet ___
14. Propel yourself back toward midcourt ___
15. Return to center court ___

How to Execute the Backhand Clear

When the shuttle is hit to your backhand side during a rally, you should move into a position behind the oncoming shuttle and assume your backhand grip. If you are returning with a backhand overhead clear, you should turn your shoulders and pivot at your waist to get sideways to the net. As the shuttle drops in the hitting area, swing your racket upward with the elbow leading the hand up to contact with the shuttle (see Figure 4.2). Contact the shuttle in front of your body and as high as possible with the racket finishing in the direction of the shuttle's trajectory. The racket face is angled upward, directing the shuttle high and deep. The defensive clear is directed upward, high over your opponent's head. The offensive clear is hit in a flat, fast trajectory, just out of your opponent's reach.

Your hand and wrist allow your racket arm to follow through naturally. Rapid forearm supination provides the majority of the power. Your racket travels through the contact area and then forward in line with the flight of the shuttle. At or very soon after contact on the backhand overhead, transfer your body weight rapidly as your feet push your body back toward midcourt.

If you are clearing from near the net, you should use an underhand stroke. Reach with the dominant arm and place the racket face under the dropping return. As the shuttle drops in the hitting area, swing your racket upward to contact the shuttle, directing it high and deep (see Figure 4.2). Contact the shuttle with your racket hand, palm down, in front of your body and as high as possible. Hit the shuttle with vigorous forearm supination directing it up, high, and deep, with the racket finishing in the direction of the shuttle's trajectory.

FIGURE
4.2

KEYS TO SUCCESS

BACKHAND CLEAR

Overhead Clear
Preparation

1. Backhand or thumb-up grip ___
2. Recover into waiting or receiving stance ___
3. Hold racket arm parallel to floor ___
4. Racket head is pointed downward ___
5. Distribute weight evenly on both feet ___

Execution

6. Reach with the dominant foot ___
7. Pivot and turn with back to net ___
8. Wrist in laid back or cocked position ___
9. Elbow leads forward swing ___
10. Racket head trails hand up to contact ___
11. Contact as high as possible ___
12. Angle racket face up and outward ___
13. Supinate forearm ___

Follow-Through

14. Continue swing upward ___
15. Racket follows flight of shuttle ___
16. Swing toward the net ___
17. Racket follows through naturally ___
18. Push off rear foot back to midcourt ___
19. Return to center court ___

Underhand Clear
Preparation

1. Backhand or thumb-up grip ___
2. Reach forward with dominant hand and foot ___
3. Hold racket arm up, palm down ___
4. Put weight slightly on front foot ___

Execution

5. Pivot and reach for the oncoming shuttle ___
6. Place racket under dropping shuttle ___
7. Put wrist in laid back or cocked position ___
8. Drop racket down and swing it quickly up to contact shuttle as high as possible ___
9. Meet shuttle as high as possible ___
10. Supinate forearm ___

Follow-Through

11. Swing up in line with shuttle's flight ___
12. Forearm rotation allows your racket to follow through naturally ___
13. Push off and propel back toward midcourt ___
14. Return to center court ___

CLEAR SHOT SUCCESS STOPPERS

Errors in performing the clear shot are apparent at all levels of badminton competition. Beginners and often the intermediate levels demonstrate poor stroke production. Practice and repetition will provide you with more success on the court.

Error	Correction
1. You have an incorrect grip.	1. Grasp your racket as if shaking hands with it. Check for "V" on top.
2. You lack full arm extension at contact resulting in loss of power.	2. Many beginners hit with a bent arm. Do not short arm your throwing motion.
3. Your preparatory position is poor.	3. Move quickly to get into the proper hitting position and make contact at the proper time. You can correct this problem with concentration and practice.

CLEAR SHOT

DRILLS

1. Underhand Clear Shadow Drill

Practice both the forehand and backhand underhand swinging motions with the racket cover on your racket. The added weight and air resistance aid in developing strength and endurance in your hitting arm.

 **Success Goal** = 30 forehand swings ___
30 backhand swings ___

 **Success Check**
- Wrist should be cocked or in laid back position ___
- Lead with your wrist and hand, racket trails on the upward swing ___
- Make the racket swish ___

2. Overhand Clear Shadow Drill

Practice both the forehand and backhand overhand clear throwing motions with the racket cover on your racket. The added weight and air resistance aid in developing strength and endurance in your hitting arm.

Success Goal = 30 forehand swings ___
30 backhand swings ___

Success Check
• Lead with your elbow ___
• Your hand leads your racket on the upward swing ___
• Shift your weight ___

3. Underhand Clear From Net

Player A throws the shuttle with an overhand toss just over the net toward Player B, who steps toward the net with his dominant foot and hits an underhand clear from his forehand or backhand side. These underhand clear returns should land between the doubles' back service line and the back boundary line. Player G should return the shuttles to Player A. Players rotate after three attempts. Player A replaces Player G, B replaces A, and G moves behind Player F, and so on until all players have been at each position.

Success Goal = 3 good attempts by all players from each position ___

Success Check
• Lead with your elbow ___
• Swing fast ___
• Place shot high and deep ___

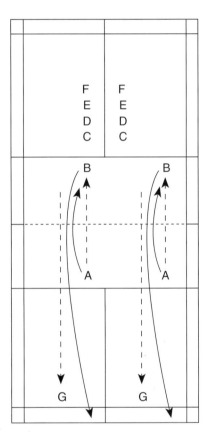

4. Serve and Clear Drill

Start with either a forehand or backhand serve, or an underhand stroking motion resulting in a high, deep clear return over your partner's head. It is not a rally so the partner serving needs to begin with five to six shuttles. This is a repetitive drill in which the server should execute at least 30 good serves or underhand clears. Partners may practice this drill simultaneously because there is no rally. Good serves need to carry over your partner's head and land near or beyond the doubles' service line in backcourt.

Success Goal = 30 good forehand serves or underhand clears ___
30 good backhand serves or underhand clears ___

Success Check
• Lead with your elbow ___
• Swing fast ___
• Place shot high and deep ___

5. Return Forehand Clear Drill

One partner sets up the other by hitting high, deep, friendly underhand serves. The receiving partner returns each serve with a forehand overhead stroking motion resulting in a high, deep clear return over her partner's head. It is not a rally so the partner setting up needs to begin with five to six shuttles. This is a repetitive drill in which the receiving partner should execute at least 30 returns before the partners reverse roles. Good returns need to land near or beyond the doubles' service line in backcourt.

 **Success Goal** = 30 good forehand clears ___

 **Success Check**
• Lead with your elbow ___
• Swing fast ___
• Place shot high and deep ___

6. Toss and Return Backhand Clear Drill

One partner sets up the other by throwing friendly, overhand tosses to her partner's backhand side close to the net. The receiving partner returns each toss with a backhand underhand stroking motion, resulting in a high, deep clear return. It is not a rally so the partner setting up needs to begin with five to six shuttles. This is a repetitive drill in which the receiving partner should execute at least 30 returns before the partners reverse roles. Good returns need to land near or beyond the doubles' service line in backcourt.

Success Goal = 30 good backhand clears ___

Success Check

• Toss bird to left and reach with your dominant hand and foot ___
• Lead with your elbow ___
• Snap the racket through the contact area ___

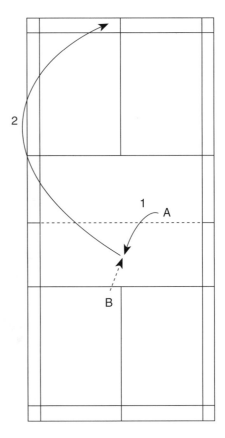

7. Overhead Clears Rally

One partner sets up the other by hitting a high, deep, friendly underhand serve. The receiving partner returns the serve with a forehand or backhand overhead stroking motion resulting in a high, deep clear return over his partner's head. This is a rally so the partner setting up needs to begin with only one or two shuttles. This is a continuous drill in which both partners should attempt to execute as many return clears as possible, keeping the rally going indefinitely. Your returns should be high and deep enough to allow your partner plenty of time to get into position. Good returns need to land near or beyond the doubles' service line in backcourt.

Success Goal = rally 30 good clears ___

Success Check
- Lead with your elbow ___
- Swing fast ___
- Direct return to partner's forehand side ___

To Increase Difficulty
- Recover to your ready position following each attempt.
- Alternate hitting forehand and backhand overhead clears.
- Run in and touch the short service line between clears and then return to your receiving position.
- Hit clears with a faster and flatter trajectory. Hit this faster, attacking clear sooner and more in front of you. Hit it high enough so your opponents cannot intercept it before it gets to the back of their court.

To Decrease Difficulty
- Have your body already turned in your sideways hitting stance either at the net or backcourt.
- Begin with your racket arm already held up and behind your head if you are in the backcourt or up and reaching forward if at the net.
- Begin with your weight already shifted to your rear foot if in the backcourt or to your front foot if at the net.
- Hit higher and shorter to give your partner more time. This also enables her to hit a deeper return to you.

8. Rotating Clears

Player A serves high to Player E and rotates to the rear of his line. Player E clears to Player B and rotates to the end of his line. Continue with each player hitting one clear and rotating to the end of the line.

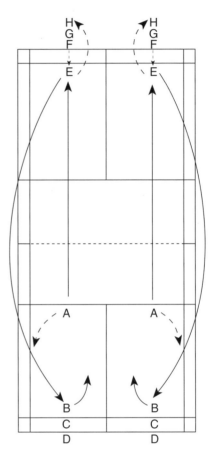

Success Goal = rally 30 good clears in succession ___

Success Check
• Lead with your elbow ___
• Swing fast ___
• Direct return to partner's forehand side ___

9. Straight and Crosscourt Clears

You can use this sequence of clears effectively for warming up before a match. Either player may begin the drill by clearing crosscourt to his partner's deep forehand. Following that initial clear, either partner must hit a clear return crosscourt or down the line. There is no set sequence of returns, except all returns must be cleared deep, whether to your partner's forehand or backhand.

**Success Goal** = rally 30 good clears in succession ___

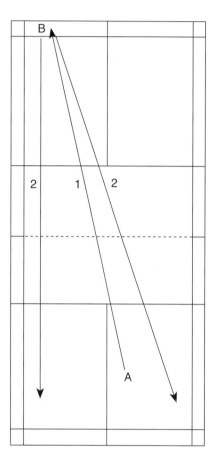

**Success Check**
• Lead with your elbow ___
• Swing fast ___
• Place shot high and deep ___

CLEAR SHOT SUCCESS SUMMARY

As you prepare to be observed and evaluated on your forehand and backhand clears, remember to prepare quickly. Make contact with the shuttle as soon as possible in front of your dominant shoulder. These strokes should have a rapid weight shift followed by a quick change of direction back to midcourt. Swing your racket arm up, leading with your elbow as you extend your arm. Allow your hand and racket to follow through naturally. Complete the stroke by pushing off and propelling yourself back to midcourt with your rear foot.

Practice the overhead and underhand clears until you have a continuous, rhythmic motion that results in an effective, accurate, and powerful stroke. When you are ready, ask someone to observe you using the "Keys to Success" checklists (see Figures 4.1-4.2) to rate your shots. Attempt to visualize each stroke and critique your thoughts out loud with your evaluator.

DROP SHOT: LOW AND SLOW

The drop shot is hit low, just over the net, and slow, so the bird drops directly down toward the floor. The bird is contacted farther in front of the body than the overhead clear, and your racket face is angled to direct the bird more downward. The shuttle is blocked rather than hit with power. The most important characteristic of a good overhead drop shot is deception. If you are deceptive enough, the drop shot may not be returned at all. The worst characteristic of the drop shot is its slow flight. Anything moving slowly, unfortunately, gives your opponent more time.

Emphasize making your preparatory motion similar to your other overhead strokes. Use a big, upper body turn even though it is not necessary for generating any power. This exaggerated shoulder rotation adds to your deception. However, because the bird is blocked or sliced rather than patted, it loses speed quickly and falls straight down after passing over the net.

Why Is the Drop Shot Important?

The value of the overhead or underhand drop shot lies in combining it with the clear to move your opponent around and force him or her to defend the entire court. To be effective, the drop shot must be accurate to make your opponents cover as much of their court as possible.

How to Execute the Forehand Drop Shot

The intention of the forehand overhead drop shot should be to suggest that you are about to hit an overhead clear or smash. The difference is primarily in your racket speed. To execute a good forehand overhead drop shot, you should assume the handshake grip and move into position behind and in line with the shuttle. As you move into position, pivot at your waist and turn your shoulders sideways to the net. Throw your racket up to meet the shuttle. Take the overhead drop shot as high as possible and out in front of your body.

Direct the shuttle downward. Swing your racket upward with your racket head leading (see Figure 5.1). Follow through in the direction of the bird's flight and finish with your racket head pointing downward. Tilt your racket face at the angle that the shuttle is to take. Hit the crosscourt drop shot with the same overhead motion except tilt the racket face slightly to hit more across the bird. This creates a slicing action similar to the slice serve in tennis and is intended to deceive your opponent. This deception or misdirection is sometimes difficult to pick up and may result in a winner. It is very important to begin your throwing motion with the shoulders turned sideways to the net. This is essential for deception. Also, do not short arm or bend the elbow during execution. This alerts your opponent that a drop shot is coming.

If you are hitting from near the net, you should use an underhand stroke. Reach with the dominant arm and place the racket face under the dropping return. As the shuttle drops in the hitting area, softly bump or lift the shuttle over as close to the top of the net as possible (see Figure 5.1). Contact the shuttle with your racket hand, palm up, in front of your body and as high as possible, directing the shuttle upward. Your racket finishes in a lifting motion in the direction of the shuttle's trajectory. The sooner you make contact, the better your results will be. You should lift from your shoulder and not from your hand or wrist. The shuttle bounces off the face of the racket and literally falls over the net from lack of speed. You may also slice or tumble the shuttle over the net to make it more difficult for your opponent to return this hairpin net drop. Another variation of the drop shot hit at the net is the push shot. Play the push shot at or above the top of the net and direct the shuttle down into your opponent's court. This is particularly effective in doubles' play when you push the shuttle past the net player and force the backcourt player to hit his return up. There may also be some indecision as to which player should make the return. The sooner and higher you contact the shuttle, the sharper and steeper your net returns will be.

How to Execute the Backhand Drop Shot

When the shuttle is hit to your backhand side during a rally, you should move into a position behind the oncoming shuttle and assume your backhand grip. If you are returning with a backhand overhead drop shot, you should turn your shoulders and pivot at your waist to get sideways to the net. As the shuttle drops in the hitting area, swing your racket upward with the elbow leading the hand up to contact the shuttle (see Figure 5.2). Contact the shuttle in front of your body and as high as possible, with the racket finishing in the direction of the shuttle's trajectory. Angle the racket face downward, directing the shuttle close to the top of the net.

Your hand and wrist allow your racket arm to follow through naturally. Forearm supination provides most of the power. Your racket travels through the contact area and then forward in line with the flight of the shuttle. However, because the bird is blocked or sliced rather than patted, it loses speed quickly and falls straight down after passing over the net. At or soon after contact on the backhand overhead drop shot, transfer your body weight rapidly as your feet push your body back toward midcourt.

If you are hitting a drop shot at the net, you should use an underhand stroke. Reach with the dominant arm and place the racket face under the dropping return. As the shuttle drops in the hitting area, lift your racket upward to contact the shuttle, bumping it just over the net (see Figure 5.2). Contact the shuttle with your racket hand, palm down, in front of your body and as high as possible. Hit the shuttle with a lifting motion from the shoulder with very little follow-through. The racket finishes in the direction of the shuttle's trajectory.

FIGURE 5.1 **KEYS TO SUCCESS**

FOREHAND DROP SHOT

Overhead Drop Shot
Preparation

1. Handshake or pistol grip ___
2. Recover into waiting or receiving stance ___
3. Hold arm up with racket head up ___
4. Distribute weight evenly on balls of feet ___

Execution

5. Reach with the dominant foot ___
6. Pivot and turn to oncoming shuttle ___
7. Backswing places wrist in cocked position ___
8. Forward swing to contact high ___
9. Racket reaches out to meet shuttle, which is blocked, not hit ___
10. Racket head travels in shuttle direction ___

Follow-Through

11. Continue in line with shuttle's flight ___
12. Swing follows angle of the shuttle ___
13. Push off with feet back toward midcourt ___
14. Return to center court ___

Underhand Drop Shot
Preparation

1. Forehand handshake, pistol grip ___
2. Reach with dominant hand and foot ___
3. Hold racket arm up ___
4. Put weight slightly on front foot ___

Execution

5. Pivot and reach in the direction of shuttle ___
6. Place racket under dropping shuttle ___
7. Put wrist in laid back or cocked position ___
8. Drop racket down and lift to contact shuttle as high as possible ___
9. Lift from shoulder; bump shuttle over net ___

Follow-Through

10. Short swing up with shuttle's flight ___
11. Racket tumbles shuttle over net ___
12. Push off with feet back toward midcourt ___

FIGURE
5.2

KEYS TO SUCCESS

BACKHAND DROP SHOT

Overhead Drop Shot
Preparation

1. Backhand or thumb-up grip ___
2. Recover into waiting or receiving stance ___
3. Hold racket arm parallel to floor ___
4. Racket head is pointed downward ___
5. Distribute weight evenly on both feet ___

Execution

6. Reach with the dominant foot ___
7. Pivot and turn back to net ___
8. Backswing places wrist in cocked position ___
9. Elbow leads forward swing ___
10. Racket head leads hand up to contact ___
11. Contact as high as possible ___
12. Angle racket face downward ___
13. Supinate forearm ___

Follow-Through

14. Continue swing down with shuttle's flight ___
15. Swing toward net ___
16. Push off rear foot back to midcourt ___
17. Return to center court ___

Underhand Drop Shot
Preparation

1. Backhand or thumb-up grip ___
2. Reach forward with dominant hand and foot ___
3. Racket arm up, palm down, racket parallel to floor ___
4. Put weight slightly on front foot ___

Execution

5. Pivot and reach in direction of shuttle ___
6. Place racket under dropping shuttle ___
7. Put wrist in laid back or cocked position ___
8. Drop racket down; lift to contact shuttle ___
9. Shoulder lift bumps shuttle over net ___

Follow-Through

10. Continue swing up with shuttle's flight ___
11. Keep firm wrist and lift from shoulder ___
12. Push off with feet back toward midcourt ___

DROP SHOT SUCCESS STOPPERS

Players at all levels of badminton competition experience problems in executing the drop shot. Practice and repetition will provide you with more success on the court.

Error	Correction
1. You use a frying pan grip.	1. Use the handshake or pistol grip.
2. You lack racket control.	2. Many beginners fail to work on their feel or touch. Practice the drop shot from backcourt and at the net.
3. You are telegraphing your drop shot.	3. Extend your racket arm completely as you reach up to make contact.
4. Your preparatory position is poor.	4. Move quickly to get into the proper hitting position and make contact as soon as possible, but under control.
5. Your reaction and movement on the court are slow.	5. Spend more time on your training and conditioning. Get in better shape and practice your footwork.

DROP SHOT

DRILLS
1. Underhand Drop Shot at Net

Player A throws the shuttle with an overhand toss just over the net toward Player B, who steps toward the net with her dominant foot and hits an underhand hairpin drop shot from her forehand or backhand side. These underhand drop shot returns should land between the short service line and the net. Player G should return the shuttles to Player A. Players rotate after three attempts. Player A takes the place of Player G, B replaces A, and G moves behind Player F, and so on until all players have been at each position.

Success Goal = 3 good attempts by all players from each position ___

Success Check
• Lead with dominant hand and arm ___
• Lift from the shoulder ___
• Bump shuttle over the net ___

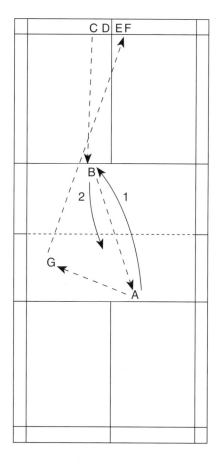

2. Crosscourt Drop Shot at Net

Player A throws the shuttle with an overhand toss just over the net toward Player B, who steps toward the net with his dominant foot and hits an underhand crosscourt drop shot from his forehand or backhand side. These underhand crosscourt drop shot returns should travel close to the top of the net and land between the short service line and the net. Player C retrieves shuttles and returns them to Player A. Players rotate after three attempts until all players have been at each position.

Success Goal = 3 good attempts by all players from each position ___

Success Check
- Lead with dominant hand and arm ___
- Lift from the shoulder ___
- Angle racket face crosscourt and push the shuttle over the net ___

3. Tumble Drop Shot at Net

Player A throws the shuttle with an overhand toss just over the net toward Player B, who steps toward the net with her dominant foot and hits an underhand tumble drop shot from her forehand or backhand side; Player C tallies the shots or returns shuttles to Player A. Keep your racket face parallel to the floor and pushed under the dropping shuttle so it will flip upside down as it makes contact and tumble as it falls. These tumble drop shot returns should fall close to the net and land well inside the short service line. Players rotate after three attempts until all players have been at each position.

Success Goal = 3 good attempts by all players from each position ___

Success Check
- Lift from the shoulder ___
- Brush shuttle with a sideways motion of the wrist ___
- Racket face slices shuttle at contact causing a tumbling action ___

4. Hairpin Drop Shot at the Net

This is a drill in which one partner begins the rally by hitting an underhand drop shot to her partner. The rally continues until one partner misses the return. This can be simply a rally drill or you may keep score. When one partner misses, the other partner gets a point. You may play games to 15 or 11 points. It does not matter which partner begins the rally. Either partner may score.

 **Success Goal** = return shuttle inside of short service line ___

Success Check
• Racket head leads ___
• Contact shuttle in front of body ___
• Racket blocks shuttle just over net ___

5. Serve and Return Overhead Drop Shot

One partner sets up the other by hitting high, deep, friendly serves. The receiving partner returns each serve with either a forehand or backhand overhead drop shot return, down and just over the net. The partner setting up is near his short service line and the receiving partner is in the backcourt, near the doubles' back service line. It is not a rally so the setting partner needs to begin with five to six shuttles. This is a repetitive drill in which the receiving partner should execute at least 30 forehand and backhand returns before the partners reverse roles. Good returns need to land between the net and the short service line on the setter's side of the court.

Success Goal = 30 good forehand drop shots ___
30 good backhand drop shots ___

Success Check
- Racket head leads ___
- Angle shuttle downward ___
- Racket blocks shuttle just over net ___

6. Drop Shot Three-Shot Rally

One partner begins the rally by setting up the other with a high, deep, friendly serve. The receiving partner returns the serve with a forehand or backhand overhead drop shot return down and just over the net. The partner setting up is near her short service line and returns the receiving partner's drop shot with an underhand drop shot at the net. It is a three-shot rally so the setting partner needs to begin with only one or two shuttles. This is a continuous drill in which each partner should execute at least 30 returns before the partners reverse roles. Good returns need to land between the net and the short service line on both sides of the court.

Success Goal = 30 good forehand drop shot rallies ___
30 good backhand drop shot rallies ___

Success Check
- Racket head leads ___
- Extend arm; contact shuttle in front of body ___
- Angle shuttle downward ___

7. Clear-Drop-Drop-Clear Continuous Rally

One partner sets up the other by hitting a high, deep, friendly underhand clear. The receiving partner returns the serve with a forehand or backhand overhead drop shot return just over the net. The server then returns this drop shot with a hairpin drop shot. The receiving partner moves into the net and returns the hairpin drop shot with an underhand clear. The rally continues indefinitely in this clear-drop-drop-clear pattern. The partner setting up needs to begin with one or two shuttles. This is a continuous drill in which the rally should continue as long as possible. Good returns need to land near or inside the short service line.

Success Goal = 30 clear-drop-drop-clears in succession ___

Success Check
• Correct grip and ready position ___
• Racket blocks shuttle close to net ___
• Able to make the rally last ___

To Increase Difficulty
• Recover to your ready position at center court following each attempt.
• Hit faster drop shots or alternate hitting crosscourt drop shots with straight ahead drops.
• Require hitter to wait in the centercourt position. Have your partner deliver a mixture of faster, crosscourt drop shots that require you to move farther and/or more quickly to make an effective return.

To Decrease Difficulty
• Have your body already turned sideways to the net in your hitting stance.
• Begin with your racket arm already held up and racket angled slightly downward.
• Begin with your weight already shifted to your nondominant foot.

8. Diagonal Drop Shot

Player A begins the rally by clearing to Player B's deep forehand or backhand side. Player B hits a diagonal or crosscourt drop shot. Player A steps in slightly and blocks the return with a straight ahead net drop shot. Player B re-drops straight ahead to Player A's side at the net. Player A crosscourt clears to Player B's deep forehand or backhand side and the rally starts over. The sequence is clear, crosscourt drop shot, net drop, net drop, crosscourt clear. This is a continuous rally to work on diagonal speed or movement on the court.

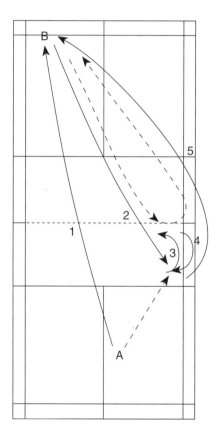

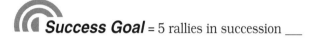 **Success Goal** = 5 rallies in succession ___

Success Check
- Racket head leads to contact shuttle in front of body ___
- Racket arm extended to angle shuttle diagonally downward ___
- Shuttle travels just over net ___

To Increase Difficulty
- Include at random a crosscourt net drop shot instead of clearing out crosscourt at the end of the sequence.
- Clear may be hit lower to give your partner less time.
- Drop shot may be hit faster to give yourself less time.

To Decrease Difficulty
- Clear may be hit higher to give your partner more time.
- Drop shot may be hit slower to give yourself more time.

DROP SHOT SUCCESS SUMMARY

Remember to prepare quickly. Pull your racket forward to make contact with the shuttle in front of your body. Swing your racket arm up with the racket head leading. Block the overhead drop shot with the racket face angled downward. Allow your hand and racket to follow through naturally. Complete the drop shot by pushing off and propelling yourself back to midcourt with your dominant foot.

Practice until the drop shot is a continuous, rhythmic motion that results in an effective, accurate, and deceptive stroke. When you are ready, ask a practice partner or instructor to use the "Keys to Success" checklists to rate your success (see Figures 5.1-5.2). Attempt to visualize each stroke and critique your thoughts out loud with your evaluator.

STEP 6

SMASH: FAST AND STEEP

The smash is hit fast, downward with force, and steep, to put away any bird that has been hit up and short. The smash can only be hit from the overhead position. The shuttle is hit with power, but you should get your timing and balance before trying to get excessive speed on your smash. The most important characteristic of a good overhead smash besides speed is your downward angle. The bird is contacted farther in front of the body than the clear or the drop shot. Your racket face is angled to direct the bird more downward. If your angle is steep enough, the smash may be unreturnable.

Several characteristics of the smash also present problems for the player doing the smashing. If the smash is returned, you will have very little time to recover. The overhead smash requires a lot of energy and can quickly tire you out. Also, the farther you are from the net, the less steep your smash will be. Therefore, it is important for you to choose the correct opportunity to use your smash most effectively.

Why Is the Smash Important?

The value of the overhead smash is that it gives your opponents very little time to prepare or return any shuttle that they have hit up and short. The smash is used extensively in doubles. High-speed motion cinematography has shown that the overhead smash loses approximately two-thirds of its initial velocity by the time it reaches your opponent on the other side of the net. The steeper the angle you can create, the less time your opponent will have to react. Also, the more accurate your smash, the more court your opponent has to cover.

How to Execute the Forehand Smash

The intention of the overhead forehand smash should be to suggest that an overhead clear or drop shot is about to be hit. The difference is primarily in your racket speed. To execute a good forehand overhead smash, you should assume the handshake grip and move into your waiting position behind and in line with the oncoming shuttle (see Figure 6.1a). As you move into position, pivot at your waist and turn your shoulders sideways to the net. Take your racket back and drop the racket head down behind your shoulder blades with your racket arm elbow pointing up.

Throw your racket up to meet the shuttle with your elbow leading. Take the overhead forehand smash as high as possible and in front of your body. Your racket head must move at a rapid rate as it goes out to meet the shuttle. Angle your racket face downward at contact (see Figure 6.1b). Keep your balance to achieve the maximum power from your shoulders, racket arm, and wrist. After contact, your forearm pronates rapidly with follow-through down and in line with the flight of the shuttle (see Figure 6.1c). Your racket head finishes pointing downward. As you complete your weight shift from back to front, your nondominant shoulder and arm assist in completing a vigorous upper body rotation and your legs' scissoring action propels you back toward center court. Even if your smash reaches speeds over 200 miles per hour, the shuttle loses speed quickly and angles down toward the floor after passing over the net.

This creates a powerful stroking action similar to the overhead smash in tennis and is intended to put away any short return by your opponent. You may push the shuttle past the net player and force the backcourt player to hit her return up, giving you or your partner an opportunity to smash. This is particularly effective in doubles' play, causing some indecision as to which player should make the return. The sooner and higher you contact the shuttle, the faster and steeper your smash returns will be.

FIGURE 6.1

KEYS TO SUCCESS

FOREHAND SMASH

Preparation

1. Handshake or pistol grip ___
2. Recover into waiting or receiving stance ___
3. Turn shoulders with feet up and back ___
4. Hold racket arm up with racket head pointed up ___
5. Distribute weight evenly on balls of feet ___

Execution

1. Put weight on rear foot ___
2. Hold nondominant arm out for balance ___
3. Backswing places wrist in cocked position ___
4. Forward swing up to contact is as high as possible ___
5. Throw racket out and upward with racket face down ___
6. Left arm aids in speeding upper body rotation ___
7. Racket head follows direction of shuttle ___

Follow-Through

1. Swing down and across body ___
2. Use scissoring action and push off with both feet ___
3. Use momentum of swing to return to center court ___

How to Execute the Backhand Smash

The intention of the overhead backhand smash should be to suggest that an overhead clear or drop shot is about to be hit. The difference is primarily in your racket speed. To execute a good overhead backhand smash, you should assume the backhand, thumb-up grip and move into your waiting position behind and in line with the oncoming shuttle (see Figure 6.2a). As you move into position, pivot at your waist and turn with your back toward the net. Take your racket back and drop the racket head down with your forearm held parallel to the floor. Your racket and thumb of your backhand grip are pointing down in this waiting position.

Throw your racket up to meet the shuttle with your elbow leading. Take the overhead backhand smash as high as possible. Your racket head must be moving at a rapid rate as it goes out to meet the shuttle. Angle your racket face downward at contact (see Figure 6.2b). Keep your balance to achieve the maximum power from your shoulders, racket arm, and wrist. After contact, your forearm supinates rapidly with your follow-through down and in line with the flight of the shuttle (see Figure 6.2c). Your racket head finishes pointing downward. Vigorous upper body rotation along with your weight shift from back to front propels you back toward center court. Your backhand smash loses speed quickly and angles down toward the floor after passing over the net.

This powerful stroking action is intended to put away any short return or to force your opponents to hit their returns up. In doubles' play, there may also be some indecision as to which player should make the return. The sooner and higher you contact the shuttle, the faster and steeper your smash returns will be.

FIGURE 6.2 **KEYS TO SUCCESS**

BACKHAND SMASH

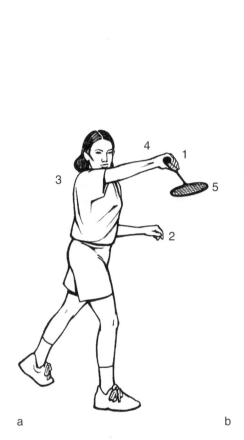

a   b   c

Preparation

1. Backhand handshake or pistol grip with thumb up ___
2. Recover into waiting or receiving stance ___
3. Turn shoulders with back toward the net ___
4. Hold racket arm up and parallel to floor ___
5. Racket head pointed downward ___
6. Distribute weight evenly on balls of feet ___

Execution

1. Put weight on your rear foot initially ___
2. Hold nondominant arm out for balance ___
3. Backswing places wrist in cocked position with thumb down ___
4. Forward swing as high as possible with racket leading ___
5. Throw racket out and upward with racket face down ___
6. Use left arm to speed rotation of upper body ___
7. Racket head follows direction shuttle is traveling ___

Follow-Through

1. Swing in line with flight of shuttle ___
2. Swing follows downward naturally ___
3. Use forearm and push off with rear foot ___
4. Use upper body swing and weight shift to return to center court ___

SMASH SUCCESS STOPPERS

Beginners and intermediate players often demonstrate incorrect technique and poor stroke production in executing the smash. Practice and repetition will provide you with better timing, balance, and success when executing the overhead smash.

Error	Correction
1. You have an incorrect grip.	1. Use the handshake or pistol grip for both the forehand and backhand smash. However, the thumb is up on backhand.
2. You lack balance.	2. Keep your left arm extended for balance.
3. Your preparation is poor.	3. Move quickly to get into your proper hitting position. Turn your shoulders with both arms up.
4. Your arm swing and resulting smash are poorly timed.	4. Spend more time on your smash and practice your stroking action so you make contact at the correct time.

SMASH

DRILLS

1. Smash Shadow Drill

Practice the forehand or backhand overhand smash motion with the racket cover on your racket. The added weight and air resistance aid in developing strength and endurance in your hitting arm.

Success Goal = 30 forehand smash swings ___

30 backhand smash swings ___

Success Check
- Hold nondominant arm up for balance ___
- Cock wrist with your elbow up, racket back and down in backswing position ___
- Lead with your wrist and hand, racket trailing on the upward swing ___

2. Self-Toss and Smash Return

Set yourself up by placing a shuttle on your racket face with your palm up. Toss the shuttle up with an underhand lift, placing the shuttle in front of the dominant shoulder, slightly in front of your body. Swing your racket up with a forehand or backhand overhead stroking motion resulting in a smash return down at your partner's feet. Both partners are situated near midcourt approximately 3 to 4 feet (about 1 meter) in front of the doubles' back service line. It is not a rally so each partner needs to begin with five or six shuttles. This is a repetitive drill in which each partner should execute at least 30 returns simultaneously. Good returns need to land near your partner's feet at midcourt.

Success Goal = 30 good forehand smashes ___

30 good backhand smashes ___

Success Check
- Racket head leads ___
- Angle shuttle downward ___
- Racket snaps through ___

3. Serve and Return Smash

One partner sets up the other by hitting high, deep, friendly underhand serves. The receiving partner returns each serve with either a forehand or backhand overhead stroking motion resulting in a smash return at her partner's feet. Both partners are situated near midcourt approximately 3 to 4 feet (about 1 meter) in front of the doubles' back service line. It is not a rally so the partner setting up needs to begin with five or six shuttles. This is a repetitive drill in which the receiving partner should execute at least 30 forehand and backhand returns before the partners reverse roles. Good returns need to land near the setting partner's feet at midcourt with no attempt to return them.

 **Success Goal** = 30 good forehand smashes ___
30 good backhand smashes ___

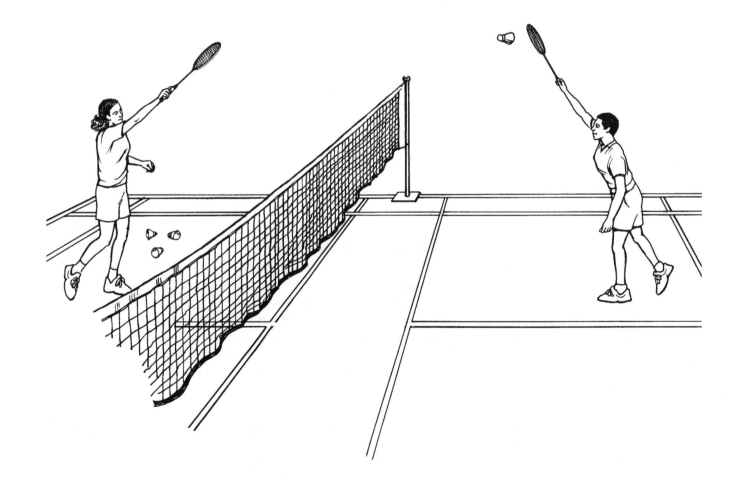 **Success Check**
• Racket head leads ___
• Contact shuttle in front of body ___
• Angle shuttle downward ___

4. Serve-Smash-Block Return

One partner begins the rally by setting up the other with a high, deep, friendly serve. The receiving partner returns the serve with a forehand or backhand overhead smash return to his partner's feet. The partner setting up is near his midcourt at the centerline and returns the receiving partner's smash with a blocked or underhand drop shot at the net. It is a three-shot rally so the setting partner needs to begin with only one or two shuttles. This is a continuous drill in which each partner should execute at least 30 serve-smash-drop shot rallies before the partners reverse roles. Good smash returns need to be angled down at your partner's feet. Good blocked drop shot returns should land between the net and the short service line on the court.

Success Goal = 30 good forehand smash-block return rallies ___
30 good backhand smash-block return rallies ___

Success Check
• Racket head leads ___
• Extend arm ___
• Racket blocks shuttle just over net on the smash return ___

5. Clear-Smash-Drop-Clear Continuous Rally

One partner sets up the other by hitting a high, deep, friendly underhand clear. The receiving partner returns the serve with a forehand or backhand overhead smash return at the serving partner's feet. The server then returns this smash with a blocked drop shot return. The receiving partner moves into the net and returns the drop shot with an underhand clear. The rally continues indefinitely in this clear-smash-drop-clear pattern. The partner setting up needs to begin with one or two shuttles. This is a continuous drill in which the rally should continue as long as possible. Good drop shot returns need to land near or inside the short service line.

Success Goal = 30 clear-forehand smash-drop-clears in succession ___
30 clear-backhand smash-drop-clears in succession ___

Success Check
- Angle smash down at partner's feet ___
- Racket blocks shuttle close to net on return of smash ___
- Able to make the rally last ___

To Increase Difficulty
- Recover to your ready position at center court following each attempt.
- Hit faster smashes or alternate hitting crosscourt drop shots with straight ahead drops.
- Touch the net before returning to your centercourt position.
- Have your partner deliver tighter, closer to the net, drop shots that require you to move farther and/or more quickly to make an effective return.
- Have your partner deliver a mixture of crosscourt drop shots that require you to move farther and/or more quickly to make an effective return.

To Decrease Difficulty
- Have your body already turned sideways to the net in your hitting stance.
- Begin with your racket arm already held up and racket angled slightly downward.
- Begin with your weight already shifted to your left foot.
- Have your partner deliver drop shot returns farther from the net that require you to move less and/or more slowly to make an effective return.
- Make drop shot returns higher in order to give your partner more time.

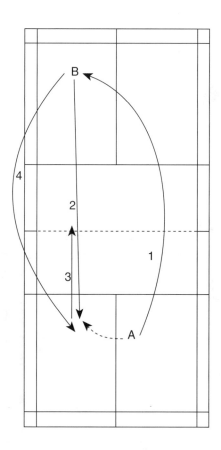

6. Smash Returns Down the Line

One partner sets up the other by hitting high, deep, friendly underhand serves to her partner. The receiving partner returns each serve with a smash return down either sideline. Both partners are situated near midcourt, approximately 3 to 4 feet (1 meter) in front of the doubles' back service line. It is not a rally so the partner setting up needs to begin with five or six shuttles. This is a repetitive drill in which the receiving partner should execute at least 30 smash returns down the sidelines before the partners reverse roles. Good returns need to land near either sideline at midcourt with no attempt to return them.

**Success Goal** = 30 good smashes ___

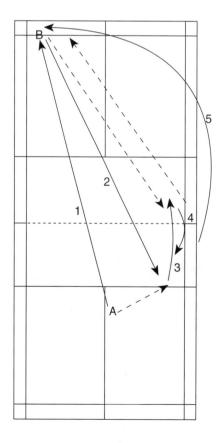**Success Check**
- Extend arm ___
- Contact shuttle in front of body on nondominant side ___
- Angle shuttle downward ___

7. Diagonal Smash

Player A begins the rally by clearing to Player B's deep forehand or backhand side. Player B hits a diagonal or crosscourt smash. Player A steps in slightly and blocks the return with a straight ahead net drop shot. Player B re-drops straight ahead to Player A's side at the net. Player A crosscourt clears to Player B's deep, forehand or backhand side and the rally starts over. The sequence is clear, crosscourt smash, drop, drop, crosscourt clear. This is a continuous rally to work on diagonal speed or movement on the court.

Success Goal = 30 clear-diagonal forehand smash-drop-drop-clears in succession ___
30 clear-diagonal backhand smash-drop-drop-clears in succession ___

Success Check
- Angle smash down at partner's feet ___
- Racket blocks shuttle close to net on return of smash ___
- Able to make the rally last ___

To Increase Difficulty
- Recover to your ready position at center court following each attempt.
- Hit faster diagonal smashes.
- Have your partner deliver tighter, closer to the net, drop shots that require you to move farther and/or more quickly to make an effective return.
- Include at random a crosscourt net drop shot instead of clearing out crosscourt at the end of the sequence. This mixture of crosscourt drop shots will require you to move farther and/or more quickly to make an effective return.

SMASH SUCCESS SUMMARY

Remember to prepare quickly. Swing your racket forward to make contact with the shuttle in front of your body. Swing your racket arm up with the racket head leading. Hit the overhead smash powerfully with the racket face angled downward. Allow your hand and racket to follow through naturally. Complete the smash by pushing off and propelling yourself back to midcourt with your dominant foot.

Practice until the overhead smash is a continuous, rhythmic motion that results in an effective, accurate, and powerful stroke. When you are ready, ask someone to observe you and check your smash stroking technique against the "Keys to Success" checklists (see Figures 6.1-6.2). Attempt to visualize each overhead smash and critique your thoughts out loud with your evaluator.

STEP

7 DRIVE: FLAT AND SIDEARM

The drive is a flat shot that directs the bird in a horizontal trajectory across the net. Both forehand and backhand drives send the shuttle just high enough to clear the net in a level or slightly downward path. Your stroking action is similar to a sidearm throwing motion and usually is played down the sidelines of your court. Your forehand and backhand drives provide a chance to work on your footwork because your stroke is generally executed between shoulder and knee height to the left or right of center court. Therefore, it emphasizes reaching for the shuttle by shuffling or sliding your feet into position.

In singles and doubles, the drive is a safe, conservative return that will keep your opponents honest and require them to lift their returns. If you hit your drive with less power, your return resembles more of a push shot or midcourt drive.

Why Is the Drive Important?

The primary objective of the drive during play is to get the shuttle over the net quickly and, with the assistance of gravity, headed for the floor. Hit it away from your opponent to force him or her to move quickly. By getting the bird below net height, your opponents will have less time and their returns will necessarily be directed upward. If you perform your drives accurately and effectively, your opponents will need to hurry to make their returns and will become more fatigued as well. A flatter, faster drive may be useful in getting the shuttle behind your opponents and potentially causing them to hit a weak return.

You may play all drives diagonally crosscourt or straight ahead down the sidelines. If you hit your drive below knee high with more power, the shuttle will be rising as it goes over the net and will continue to travel up into your opponents' court, giving them

the advantage. A slower paced, midcourt drive that reaches its peak at the net and descends from there is particularly valuable in doubles when you do not want to hit the bird up to your opponent.

How to Execute the Forehand Drive

When the shuttle is returned between shoulder and knee height to the forehand side of your centercourt position, the forehand drive becomes one of your return options. From your ready position and with your handshake grip, any low return to your forehand stresses reaching for the shuttle with your dominant arm and leg. If you are hitting a drive return, you should pivot on your nondominant foot and turn your shoulders as you reach to your side with your dominant arm and leg. Draw your racket arm back in a sidearm, backswing motion by flexing your elbow and cocking your wrist (see Figure 7.1a). Your backswing and handshake grip place the racket parallel to the floor with your palm up. As you swing your racket arm forward, put your body weight on your dominant foot. Your racket arm extends, rolls your forearm over, and contacts the shuttle as the wrist uncocks (see Figure 7.1b). Your racket foot should be pointing toward the sideline. Flex your racket leg to enable you to extend and push off back toward center court. Strike the shuttle in front of your racket foot at the highest possible point and well away from your body so your swing is not restricted. Elbow extension, forearm rotation, and wrist action provide the proper sequence of action.

Your hand and wrist allow your racket arm to follow through naturally. Rapid forearm pronation provides most of your power. Your racket travels through the contact area and then forward in the direction of the flight of the shuttle (see Figure 7.1c). Your forearm continues to pronate on your forehand drive and finishes palm down. At or soon after contact, transfer your body weight rapidly as your racket leg and foot push your body back toward midcourt.

FIGURE 7.1

KEYS TO SUCCESS

FOREHAND DRIVE

a

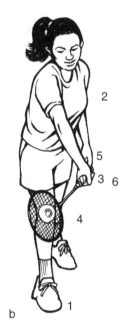

b

c

Preparation

1. Handshake or pistol grip ___
2. Recover into waiting or receiving stance ___
3. Hold racket arm up and in front of chest ___
4. Distribute weight evenly on both feet ___

Execution

1. Reach with dominant foot ___
2. Pivot and turn in direction of oncoming shuttle ___
3. Backswing places wrist in cocked position, palm up ___
4. Forward swing led by elbow, contact as high as possible ___
5. Forearm supination provides power ___
6. Hand and wrist roll over ___

Follow-Through

1. Continue swing upward in line with shuttle flight ___
2. Swing toward net naturally ___
3. Finish with palm down ___
4. Push off with foot ___
5. Use momentum of swing to return to center court ___

How to Execute the Backhand Drive

When the shuttle is returned between shoulder and knee height to the backhand side of your centercourt position, the backhand drive becomes one of your return options. From your ready position and with your backhand handshake grip, any low return to your backhand stresses a pivot and crossover step, reaching for the shuttle with your dominant arm and leg. If you are hitting a backhand drive return, you should pivot on your nondominant foot and turn your shoulders as you reach to your backhand side with your dominant arm and leg. Draw your racket arm behind your body by flexing your elbow and cocking your wrist (see Figure 7.2a). Your backswing and backhand grip place the racket parallel to the floor with your palm down. As your racket arm swings forward, transfer your body weight to your dominant foot. Point this racket foot toward the sideline. Flex your racket leg to enable you to push off toward center court. Extend your racket arm, roll your forearm over, and contact the shuttle as the wrist uncocks (see Figure 7.2b). Strike the shuttle in front of your racket foot at the highest possible point and well away from your body so your swing is not restricted. Elbow extension, forearm rotation, and wrist action provide the proper sequence of action.

Your hand and wrist allow your racket arm to follow through naturally. Rapid forearm supination provides most of the power. Your racket travels through the contact area and then forward in the direction of the flight of the shuttle (see Figure 7.2c). Your forearm continues to supinate on your backhand drive and finishes palm up. At or soon after contact, transfer your body weight rapidly as your racket leg and foot push your body back toward midcourt.

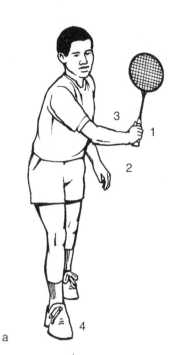

FIGURE 7.2

KEYS TO SUCCESS

BACKHAND DRIVE

Preparation

1. Handshake or pistol, back-hand thumb-up grip ___
2. Recover into waiting or receiving stance ___
3. Hold racket arm up and in front of chest ___
4. Distribute weight evenly on both feet ___

Execution

1. Reach with dominant foot ___
2. Pivot and turn in direction of oncoming shuttle ___
3. Dominant elbow is flexed ___
4. Backswing places wrist in cocked position, palm down ___
5. Forward swing led by elbow, contact as high as possible ___
6. Forearm supination provides power ___
7. Hand and wrist roll over ___

Follow-Through

1. Continue swing upward in line with shuttle flight ___
2. Swing toward net naturally ___
3. Finish with palm up ___
4. Push off with foot ___
5. Use momentum of swing to return to center court ___

DRIVE SUCCESS STOPPERS

Common faults are apparent at all levels of badminton play. Repetition and practice will assist you in developing good stroke production in the drive shot for more success in badminton.

Error	Correction
1. You have an incorrect grip.	1. Use the handshake or pistol grip. Keep thumb up on the backhand.
2. You lack full arm extension at contact and hold shuttle too close to your body.	2. Make contact well away from the body so your swing is not restricted.
3. You sometimes hit drives with too much wrist flexion; wrist snap is a misnomer; forearm rotation is more correct.	3. Move quickly to get into the proper hitting position and make contact at the proper time. Your technique and timing can be improved with concentration and practice.
4. You have lack of pace on your returns.	4. Lead with your elbow bent and your forearm parallel to the floor. Extend your arm and snap the racket through.

DRIVE

DRILLS

1. Drive Shadow Drill

Practice the forehand and backhand drive swinging motions with the racket cover on your racket. The added weight and air resistance aid in developing strength and endurance in your hitting arm. Make your racket swish.

Success Goal = 30 forehand drive swings ___
30 backhand drive swings ___

✔ **Success Check**
- Drive sidearm swinging motion ___
- Put wrist in cocked or in laid back position on your backswing ___
- Lead with your elbow, racket trailing on the forward swing ___
- Finish palm down on forehand and palm up on backhand ___

2. Push or Drive Return From Midcourt

Player A tosses or hits the shuttle near midcourt toward Player B, who steps toward the sideline with her dominant foot and hits a sidearm push or drive shot from her forehand side. These push or drive shot returns should land near midcourt between the back boundary line and the net. Player C should return the shuttles to Player A. Players rotate after three attempts until all players have been at each position. Repeat drill on your backhand side.

Success Goal = 3 good attempts by all players from each position ___

Success Check
• Lead with dominant foot and elbow ___
• Extend the racket arm from the elbow ___
• Push the shuttle over the net down the sideline near midcourt ___

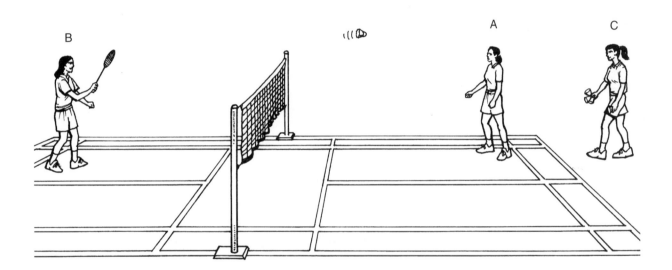

3. Crosscourt Drive Shot at Net

Player A throws the shuttle with an overhand toss near midcourt toward Player B, who steps toward the sideline with his dominant foot and hits a diagonal, crosscourt push or drive shot from his forehand or backhand side. These sidearm, crosscourt push or drive returns should travel close to the top of the net and land between the short service line and the back boundary line near midcourt. Player G should return the shuttles to Player A. Players rotate after three attempts. Player A takes the place of Player G, B replaces A, and G moves behind Player F, and so on until all players have been at each position.

Success Goal = 3 good attempts by all players from each position ___

Success Check
• Lead with dominant leg and arm ___
• Extend from the elbow allowing forearm rotation ___
• Angle racket face crosscourt and push or drive the shuttle, flat toward midcourt ___

4. Toss and Hit Drive

Each partner sets herself up by tossing a shuttle to her forehand or backhand side. It is not a rally so you need to begin with five or six shuttles. This is a repetitive drill in which each partner should execute at least 30 drive returns, with her partner doing the same from the opposite side of the net. Good returns need to land near or beyond your partner's position on the opposite side of the net.

Success Goal = 30 forehand drives ___
30 backhand drives ___

**Success Check**

- Push off and reach with your dominant hand and foot ___
- Snap the racket through the contact area with forearm pronation ___
- Finish with your hand palm down on forehand and palm up on backhand ___
- Hit flat and quick ___

5. Return With Drive

One partner sets up the other by hitting flat, friendly, midcourt drives. The receiving partner returns each drive with either a forehand or backhand drive. It is not a rally so the partner setting up needs to begin with five or six shuttles. This is a repetitive drill in which the receiving partner should execute at least 30 returns before the partners reverse roles. Good returns need to land near or beyond your partner's position at midcourt.

Success Goal = 30 good forehand drives ___
30 good backhand drives ___

Success Check

- Elbow leads with palm up initially ___
- Pronate forearm, finish palm down ___
- Hit flat and sidearm ___

6. Drive Four-Way Rally

This rally begins with four players on a court. Partners face each other on opposite sides of the net. Partner A sets up Partner B by pushing or driving a flat, friendly, midcourt forehand drive down the line. Partner B returns the drive with a backhand drive to Partner A. Partner C sets up Partner D by pushing or driving a flat, friendly, midcourt forehand drive down the line. Partner D returns the drive with a backhand drive to Partner C. These are rallies so each partner needs to begin with only one or two shuttles. It is a continuous drill in which all partners should attempt to execute as many drive returns as possible, keeping the rally going indefinitely. Your returns should be flat and near enough to your partner to allow the rally to continue. Good returns should be sent directly back at your partner near midcourt.

Success Goal = 20 to 30 good flat-flat drive rallies ___

✔ Success Check

- Lead with your elbow ___
- Swing fast, quick flat-flat exchanges ___
- Direct return toward partner's body ___

To Increase Difficulty

- Recover to your ready position following each attempt.
- Shuffle sideways and touch the centerline between drives and then return to your ready position.
- Hit drives with a faster and flatter trajectory. Hit this quick, flat drive slightly sooner and more in front of you. This flat-flat-flat exchange may be so fast that you do not have time to step, but only to turn your hips and maneuver the racket quickly from forehand to backhand depending on your partner's pace and direction.

To Decrease Difficulty

- Have your body already turned in your sideways hitting stance for either forehand or backhand drives from midcourt.
- Begin with your racket arm already held in your backswing position before attempting the forehand or backhand drive.
- Begin with your weight already shifted to your dominant leg and foot and with your racket arm already in your backswing position.

7. Continuous Drive Rally

One partner sets up the other by pushing or driving a flat, friendly, midcourt drive. The receiving partner returns the drive with a forehand or backhand drive to his partner. This is a rally so the partner starting needs to begin with only one or two shuttles. It is a continuous drill in which both partners should attempt to execute as many drive returns as possible, keeping the rally going indefinitely. Your returns should be flat and near enough to your partner to allow the rally to continue. Good returns should be sent directly back at your partner near midcourt.

 **Success Goal** = 20 to 30 good flat-flat drive rallies ___

✔ **Success Check**
• Lead with your elbow ___
• Swing fast, quick flat-flat exchanges ___
• Direct return toward partner's body ___

To Increase Difficulty
• Recover to your ready position following each attempt.
• Alternate hitting forehand and backhand overhead drives.
• Shuffle sideways and touch the singles' sideline between drives and then return to your ready position.
• Hit drives with a faster and flatter trajectory. Hit this quick, flat drive slightly sooner and more in front of you. This flat-flat-flat exchange may be so fast that you do not have time to step, but only to turn your hips and maneuver the racket quickly from forehand to backhand depending on your partner's pace and direction.

To Decrease Difficulty
• Have your body already turned in your sideways hitting stance for either forehand or backhand drives from midcourt.
• Begin with your racket arm already held in your backswing position before attempting the forehand or backhand drive.
• Begin with your weight already shifted to your dominant leg and foot and with your racket arm already in your backswing position.

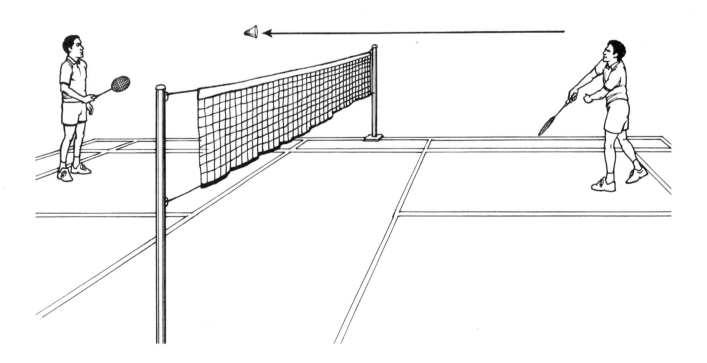

8. Alternate Sideline and Crosscourt Drives

Player A will hit only down the line drive shot returns and Player B will hit only crosscourt drive shot returns. Player A begins by pushing or driving a flat, friendly, midcourt drive down the sideline to Player B's backhand. Player B returns the drive with a crosscourt drive to Player A's backhand side. Player A then pushes or drives his return down the sideline. Player B then hits a forehand drive crosscourt. This is a rally so the partner starting up needs to begin with only one or two shuttles. It is a continuous drill in which both partners should attempt to execute as many drive returns as possible, keeping the rally going indefinitely. Your returns should be flat and near enough to your partner to allow the rally to continue. Good returns should be sent either down the sideline or crosscourt near midcourt. Each rally should consist of approximately 20 to 30 good drive shot exchanges. Then you should change the sequence to allow Player A to hit crosscourt and Player B to hit down the sideline.

Success Goal = 20 to 30 good flat-flat drive rallies ___

Success Check
- Elbow leads arm extension followed by forearm rotation ___
- Swing under control, pushing or directing the shuttle to midcourt ___
- Hit flat crosscourt and down the sideline exchanges ___

DRIVE SUCCESS SUMMARY

As you prepare to be observed and evaluated on your forehand and backhand drives, use the correct grips and prepare quickly. Make contact with the shuttle out to your side as soon as possible in front of your dominant foot or leg. Your footwork for these strokes requires a rapid shuffle and reach, followed by a quick change of direction back to midcourt. Swing your racket arm out and lead with your elbow as you swing your arm in a sidearm throwing motion. Allow your hand and racket to follow through naturally. Emphasize vigorous forearm rotation, finishing palm down on your forehand drive and palm up on your backhand drive. Complete the stroke by pushing off and propelling yourself back to midcourt with your dominant foot.

Practice the forehand and backhand drives until you have a fast, whiplike motion that results in an effective and accurate stroke. When you are ready, ask a trained partner to observe you and analyze your drive using the "Keys to Success" checklists (see Figures 7.1-7.2). Attempt to visualize each stroke and discuss your thoughts out loud with your evaluator.

STEP 8

AROUND THE HEAD STROKE: QUICK AND FLEXIBLE

The around the head stroke requires you to hit the shuttle over your nondominant shoulder. This around the head stroking motion provides a quick, strong return and is often used instead of the backhand, particularly in doubles. Many female players prefer the around the head stroke over the full backhand. In singles' play, it may be used to return from the backhand side, especially to intercept and quickly return a low clear in that area.

The around the head swing requires you to get closer to the shuttle and thus to move more quickly than you would on your backhand return. Also, as you execute the around the head stroke, your nondominant leg and foot absorb a tremendous amount of shock and impact. A player landing from this jumping action absorbs shock three to four times body weight, and exposes the ankle, foot, and leg to the danger of strain or sprain.

Why Is the Around the Head Stroke Important?

The around the head stroke allows you to make returns from your backhand side without hitting a backhand. The stroke is generally more powerful than the backhand and is similar to hitting your forehand stroke around and over your nondominant shoulder. However, it does require more energy and possibly a faster initial movement to execute successfully. You may use the around the head clear, drop shot, smash, and drive to return shots from the backhand side. It is more often used in doubles' play because it typically gets back to your opponents faster, giving them less reaction time. The around the head stroke requires you to get closer to the oncoming shuttle and thus takes you out of center court. But in doubles, you have a partner to help so complete recovery is not always necessary.

How to Execute the Around the Head Stroke

When hitting over your nondominant shoulder, bend your body slightly toward your backhand side with your weight shifted primarily to your nondominant foot. Your handshake grip saves time and is very effective in returning low, flat shots in that area (see Figure 8.1a). Hit the shuttle over your nondominant shoulder at the highest possible point.

Bend your body toward your backhand side as you shift your weight to your nondominant foot (see Figure 8.1b). Swing the racket around behind your head, reaching with your racket arm and pulling your racket forward to intercept the shuttle over the nondominant shoulder. Shoulder flexibility is very important here. Your forearm almost brushes your head on your forward swing. At or soon after contact, transfer your body weight rapidly as your nondominant foot pushes your body back toward midcourt. Your hand and wrist allow your racket arm to follow through naturally. Rapid forearm pronation provides most of the power. Your racket travels through the contact area and then forward in line with the flight of the shuttle (see Figure 8.1c).

FIGURE 8.1

KEYS TO SUCCESS

AROUND THE HEAD

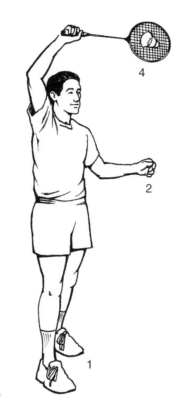

a

b

c

Preparation

1. Handshake or pistol grip ___
2. Waiting or receiving stance ___
3. Hold racket arm up with racket head pointed up ___
4. Put weight on front or nondominant foot ___

Execution

1. Dominant leg pushes to nondominant ___
2. Bend body toward backhand ___
3. Backswing takes racket behind head ___
4. Forward swing to contact over left shoulder ___
5. Pronate forearm ___
6. Racket head follows through ___

Follow-Through

1. Continue swing in line with shuttle's flight ___
2. Swing toward net naturally ___
3. Nondominant foot absorbs impact from weight shift ___
4. Push off with nondominant foot to propel back to midcourt ___

AROUND THE HEAD STROKE SUCCESS STOPPERS

Errors in executing the around the head stroke are apparent at all levels of badminton competition. Practice and repetition will provide you with more consistency and success on the court.

Error	Correction
1. You have an incorrect grip.	1. Use the handshake or pistol grip.
2. You lack shoulder flexibility.	2. Many beginners fail to work on their flexibility. Incorporate stretching exercises into your daily routine.
3. Your preparatory position is poor.	3. Move quickly to get into the proper hitting position and make contact at the proper time. You can generally correct this problem with concentration and practice.
4. You are slow to recover after hitting the around the head stroke.	4. As the shot is made and your nondominant foot hits the floor, push off toward midcourt.

AROUND THE HEAD STROKE

DRILLS

1. Around the Head Shadow Drill

Practice the around the head throwing motion with the racket cover on your racket. The added weight and air resistance aid in developing strength and endurance in your hitting arm. Make your racket swish.

**Success Goal** = 30 around the head swings ___

Success Check
• Around the head swing ___
• Brush your head with your arm ___
• Brush your shoulder with your racket ___

2. Landing and Recovery Drill

Practice the around the head motion emphasizing the push off your dominant foot with the subsequent landing and change of direction with your nondominant foot. You can use a mirror to give you visual feedback. If this is not possible, practice this movement on the court. Begin in your ready or receiving position. Propel yourself backward, pushing off with your dominant foot and landing on your nondominant foot, followed by a quick change of direction back to your dominant foot.

**Success Goal** = 30 around the head stroke swings, landings, and push offs ___

Success Check
• Shift weight ___
• Bounce back ___
• Swing fast ___

3. Around the Head Shot Returns

One partner sets up the other by hitting relatively flat but friendly shots to her partner's backhand. The receiving partner returns each of these with an around the head stroking motion resulting in either clears, drives, drop shots, or smashes. The partner setting up is near midcourt and the receiving partner is also near her midcourt. It is not a rally so your serving partner needs to begin with five or six shuttles. This is a repetitive drill in which the receiving partner should execute at least 30 returns before the partners reverse roles. Good returns need to land near the doubles' back service line or the back boundary line on the setter's side of the court. Repeat this rally with clear and drop return shots.

Success Goal = 30 good around the head drive shots ___
30 good around the head clear shots ___
30 good around the head drop shots ___
30 good around the head smashes ___

Success Check

- Backswing takes racket around behind your head ___
- Point elbow above your dominant shoulder ___
- Contact over your nondominant shoulder ___

To Increase Difficulty

- Recover to your ready position following each attempt.
- Alternate hitting crosscourt and down the line.
- Wait in the receiving position. Have your partner deliver a mixture of drive and flick serves that require you to intercept and/or move quickly to make an effective around the head return of serve.

To Decrease Difficulty

- Have your body already bent or leaning toward your backhand.
- Begin with your racket arm already held up and behind your head.
- Begin with your weight already shifted to your nondominant foot.

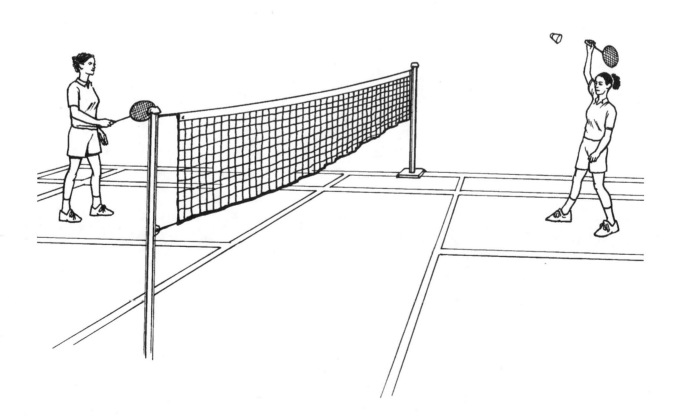

4. Around the Head Drop-Clear Rally

Partner A sets up Partner B by hitting relatively flat but friendly shots to his backhand. Partner B returns each of these with an around the head stroking motion resulting in a drop shot return just over the net. Partner A begins near midcourt and walks in toward the net after hitting his initial clear. Partner B also begins near midcourt, but may have to move toward backcourt to hit his around the head stroke. It is a rally so Partner A needs to begin with only one or two shuttles. This is a continuous drill in which Partner B should execute at least 30 drop shot returns followed by flat clears before the partners reverse roles. Good returns need to land near the net and inside the short service line on the setter's side of the court. Partner A should remain at the net and hit flat, low clears to Partner B and attempt to make the drill continuous. Repeat this drill using clear and drive return rallies.

Success Goal = 30 good around the head drop shots ___
30 good around the head clear shots ___
30 good around the head drive shots___

Success Check
- Backswing takes racket around behind your head ___
- Point elbow above your dominant shoulder ___
- Contact over your nondominant shoulder ___

To Increase Difficulty
- Recover to your ready position following each attempt.
- Alternate hitting crosscourt and down the line.
- Wait in the receiving position. Have your partner deliver a mixture of drive and flick serves that require you to intercept and/or move quickly to make an effective around the head return of serve.

To Decrease Difficulty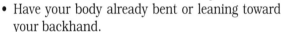
- Have your body already bent or leaning toward your backhand.
- Begin with your racket arm already held up and behind your head.
- Begin with your weight already shifted to your nondominant foot.

5. Setup Around the Head Drive-Clear Rally

Partner A sets up Partner B by hitting relatively flat but friendly shots to his backhand. Partner B returns each of these with a drive or clear to Partner A's midcourt, using an around the head stroking motion. Partner A remains near midcourt after hitting his initial clear. Partner B also begins near midcourt, but may have to move toward backcourt in order to hit the around the head stroke. This is a rally, so Partner A needs to begin with only one or two shuttles. Try to make good returns to your partner's backhand side of the court. Both partners should remain near midcourt and hit flat, low clears and try to keep the rally going.

Success Goal = 30 good around the head drive shots ___
30 good around the head clear shots ___

Success Check
• Contact over your nondominant shoulder ___
• Shuttle travels toward each partner's backhand side near center court ___
• Shift weight and recover ___

To Increase Difficulty
• Recover to your ready position following each attempt.
• Alternate hitting around the head clears and drives.
• Wait in the receiving position. Have your partner deliver a mixture of flat and high returns that require you to intercept or move quickly to make an effective around the head stroke.

To Decrease Difficulty
• Bend your body or lean toward your backhand side.
• Begin with your racket arm held up and behind your head.
• Begin with your weight shifted to your left foot.

6. Diagonal Around the Head Smash

Player A begins the rally by clearing to Player B's deep backhand side. Player B hits a diagonal or around the head crosscourt smash. This is sometimes referred to as a *reverse smash*. Player A steps in slightly and blocks the return with a straight-ahead net drop shot. Player B drops straight ahead to Player A's backhand side at the net. Player A crosscourt clears to Player B's deep backhand side, and the rally starts over. The sequence is clear, crosscourt smash, drop, drop, crosscourt clear. Work on this continuous rally to improve diagonal speed and movement on the court.

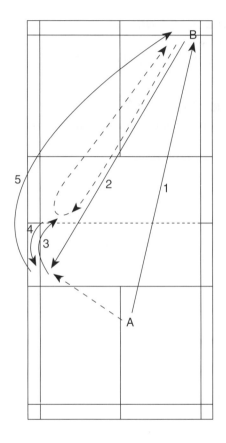

Success Goal = 5 rallies in succession __

Success Check
• Smash angled down at partner's feet __
• Racket blocks shuttle close to net on return of smash __
• Able to make the rally last __

To Increase Difficulty
• Clear the return from the net lower, thus allowing less time to recover.
• Include a crosscourt net drop shot instead of clearing out crosscourt at the end of the sequence.

To Decrease Difficulty
• Hit a half-smash or smash with less power to provide yourself more time to recover.
• Clear the return from the net higher, thus allowing more time to recover.

7. Around the Head Reverse Drop Shot

Player A begins a rally by clearing to Player B's deep backhand side. Player B hits a diagonal, or around the head, crosscourt drop shot. This is sometimes called a *reverse drop shot*. Player A steps into the net and blocks the return with a straight-ahead net drop shot. Player B drops straight ahead to Player A's backhand side at the net. The rally continues as Player A clears crosscourt to Player B's deep backhand side. The sequence is clear, around the head crosscourt drop shot, straight drop, straight drop, crosscourt clear. Work on this continuous rally to improve diagonal speed and movement on the court.

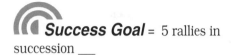

Success Goal = 5 rallies in succession ___

Success Check

• Drop shot angled down and travels close to the net ___
• Racket blocks shuttle close to net on return of reverse drop shot ___
• Able to keep the rally going ___

To Increase Difficulty

• Return straight drop shots as tight hairpin drop shots or tumble drop shots.
• Hit a fast drop shot or the reverse drop shot with more power to give yourself less time to recover.
• Clear the return from the net lower to give yourself less time to recover.
• Include a crosscourt net drop shot instead of clearing out crosscourt at the end of the sequence.

To Decrease Difficulty

• Hit the reverse drop shot with less power to give yourself more time to recover.
• Clear the return from the net higher to give yourself more time to recover.

8. Around the Head Returns

Player A initiates the drill with either a drive or flick serve to Player B's backhand. Player B returns the serve with either an around the head clear, drop shot, smash, or drive. This is not a rally, so Player A should begin with five or six shuttles. It is a repetitive drill in which one partner should execute at least 30 good around the head returns. A mixture of clear, drop shot, smash, and drive returns should be successfully completed before the partners reverse roles.

Success Goal = 30 good around the head returns of flick serves ___
30 good around the head returns of drive serves ___

✔ Success Check

• Receiver holds racket chest high and in front of the nondominant shoulder ___
• Receiver begins in a staggered stance with nondominant foot up and dominant foot back ___
• Contact over nondominant shoulder ___

To Increase Difficulty

• Move your receiving position closer to the short service line.

To Decrease Difficulty

• Move your receiving position farther from the short service line.
• Alter your receiving stance so that your nondominant foot is back and your dominant foot is up.

AROUND THE HEAD SUCCESS SUMMARY

As you prepare to be observed and evaluated on your around the head stroke, remember to take your racket back quickly. Pull your racket forward to make contact with the shuttle over your left shoulder. The around the head stroke should have a rapid weight shift from right to left, followed by a quick change of direction back to midcourt. Swing your racket arm around behind your head with your forearm almost brushing your head as you extend your arm. Allow your hand and racket to follow through naturally. Complete the stroke by pushing off and propelling yourself back to midcourt with your left foot.

Practice until the around the head stroke is a continuous, rhythmic motion that results in an effective, accurate, and powerful stroke. When you are ready, ask a coach or instructor to observe you and check your stroke using the "Keys to Success" checklist (see Figure 8.1). Attempt to visualize each stroke and critique your thoughts out loud with your evaluator.

STEP 9

SINGLES' PLAY: FITNESS AND PATIENCE

Singles' play is generally a game of fitness and patience. You are responsible for your good and bad shots. Your success or failure usually depends on your ability to sustain the rally and maneuver your opponent around the court until she hits a weak return. As a beginner, the clear and drop shot are the shots you will use most often to accomplish this task. Your primary objective is to keep the rally going. Advanced badminton players add the smash, the drive, and the around the head shots, along with variation and greater skill in their execution. They learn to sustain the rally even with better players and dictate their opponents' returns to a great extent.

Changes in the pace and the location of your serve are also important. You should develop your skill in executing the attacking clear, the fast drop shot, and the half smash if the situation requires it. The quality of your strokes and your ability to execute them under pressure during game play determine whether you win or lose. Accuracy and deception in your shot making, along with good reflexes and endurance, greatly increase your ability to cover your court in singles' play.

Singles' play in badminton provides the opportunity to succeed or fail in competition on your terms. Badminton singles is also an excellent form of aerobic exercise and is beneficial in improving your cardiovascular conditioning and overall health. Other rewards exist in the forms of recreational, sociological, and psychological benefits, as well as tangible awards, such as trophies, medals, rankings, and so forth.

How to Become a Good Singles' Player

One of the most important aspects of singles' play is your ability to make decisions during a rally. Your ability to execute the numerous shots accurately and consistently is sometimes referred to as stroke production. You can improve your stroke production by practicing certain situations or a specific sequence of action. Another means of improving your singles' game is to observe successful players and critique their play. Note weaknesses that are common to most players or tendencies they might have from certain areas of their court. You can determine some weaknesses by scouting a potential opponent before playing against him or during your warm-up before playing your match. You should take advantage of any discernible weakness in your opponent's game.

To be successful, beginners must learn to sustain a rally in singles' play. Most beginners have not learned to slice or cut their returns, to tumble the bird at the net, or to use much deception. Therefore, strategy for a beginner is very basic. Try to outlast or outsteady your opponent. Keep the shuttle in play and wait for your opponent to make a mistake. A good way to help improve your steadiness is to hit high, deep returns and to give yourself plenty of margin for error at the net. Other important elements of strategy to develop after gaining some degree of racket control are

- to hit most birds deep into your opponent's court;
- to hit most returns to your opponent's weaker side, which is usually her backhand;
- to move your opponent around the court by hitting the bird from side to side and up and back;
- to emphasize placement and depth rather than speed on your returns, which should result in fewer errors;
- to change the pace during play;
- to never change a winning strategy and to always change a losing strategy; and
- to make all your overhead strokes look the same because deception is a key part of becoming a better player.

SINGLES' PLAY SUCCESS STOPPERS

Tactics or strategy are deliberate efforts by you or your opponent to either win points or regain your serve. For your strategy to be effective, you must play to your strengths and away from your opponent's strengths, if possible. If your opponent lacks speed or endurance, attempt to make him run to tire him out. Since most players do not have as strong a backhand as they do a forehand, hit the majority of your shots to his backhand. If you are not very fit, try to attack quickly and make your rallies as short as possible by smashing or hitting outright winners. You should be aggressive on your serve and safer, more conservative, on your opponent's serve. Also, learn the singles' boundaries well so you do not play any of your opponent's returns that would have been out.

Error	Correction
1. You fail to return to center court.	1. As soon as you make your return, recover to your center court.
2. You fail to make your opponent move.	2. Your every return should have the objective of moving your opponent out of her center court.
3. Your return of serve is poor; your opponent scores too easily.	3. Return your opponent's serve with a purpose, but make it a safe return that makes him move and gives you time.
4. Your serve does not work; you have difficulty scoring points.	4. Vary the speed and placement of your serve. Mix in some short, drive, or flick serves as a change of pace. Try not to let your opponent get comfortable on your serve.
5. Your stroke production is poor; you can't sustain a rally.	5. Use all four corners of your opponent's court for your returns, but give yourself plenty of room for error. When in doubt, clear!

DRILLS

1. Six on Six Clears and Drops

Six players at the net rally with net drop shots as shown by Players A and B. Six players stand near backcourt and rally with straight ahead clears as shown by Players C and D.

Success Goal = 30 good clears or drop shots in succession ___

Success Check
- Recover to your ready position after each shot ___
- Hit clears high and deep ___
- Rebound drop shots close to the top of the net ___

To Decrease Difficulty
- Give your partner more time by hitting clears higher or net drop shots higher.
- Do not tumble your drop shot returns.

2. Three on Three Clears and Drops

Players A and B rally straight ahead with clears and move from center court to backcourt following each stroke. Players C and D practice hairpin net shots.

Success Goal = 30 good clears or drop shots in succession ___

✔ Success Check

- Recover to your ready position after each shot ___
- Hit clears high and deep ___
- Rebound drop shots close to the top of the net ___

To Increase Difficulty

- Give your partner less time by hitting clears lower or net drop shots closer to net.
- Tumble your drop shot returns.

To Decrease Difficulty

- Give your partner more time by hitting clears higher or net drop shots higher.
- Do not tumble your drop shot returns.

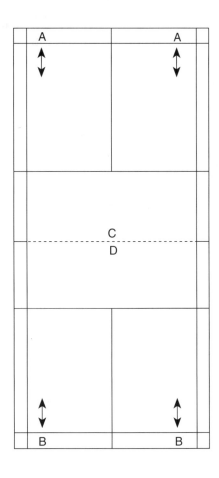

3. Forehand Clear and Backhand Drop

Player B serves high to Player A's deep forehand corner. Player A returns the serve with a straight ahead clear to Player B's deep backhand corner. Player B returns this clear with a straight ahead backhand drop shot. Player A moves into the net and returns the drop shot with an underhand clear to Player A's deep, forehand corner, and they repeat the sequence.

Success Goal = 30 good forehand clears and backhand drop shots in succession ___

Success Check

• Recover to your ready position after each shot ___
• Hit clears high and deep ___
• Let drop shots fall close to the top of the net ___

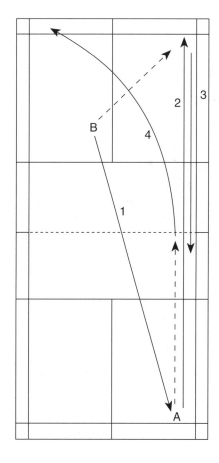

4. Four-Shot Rally

Player A serves high to Player B, who hits a straight ahead drop shot. Player C is stationed at the net and returns the drop shot with a hairpin net drop shot. Player D attempts to put this net shot away by hitting it down toward the floor. Player E retrieves and returns the shuttle to Player A. Repeat the sequence four times, alternating serves from the right service court to the left service court twice. Then rotate your positions. Player A becomes the receiver and Player E the server. Player B moves into the net and Player C remains at the net but on the opposite side. Player D is now stationed in the backcourt and retrieves the shuttles for Player E to serve. Repeat the four-shot rally sequence four times and rotate again.

Success Goal = 3 four-shot rallies out of 4 attempts in succession ___

Success Check
- Use proper footwork ___
- Hit clears high and deep ___
- Rebound drop shots close to the top of the net ___

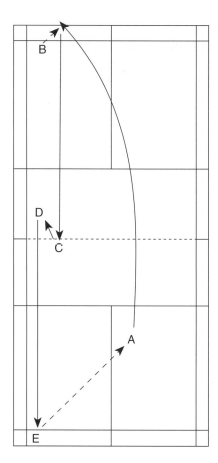

5. Three-Shot Continuous Rally

Player A begins the rally with an underhand clear to Player B's deep forehand corner. Player B returns this clear with a straight ahead drop shot or smash to Player A's backhand at the net. Player A returns this shot with a straight ahead net drop shot. Player B then clears deep to Player A's deep forehand corner, and they repeat the three-shot sequence: clear, drop/smash, drop.

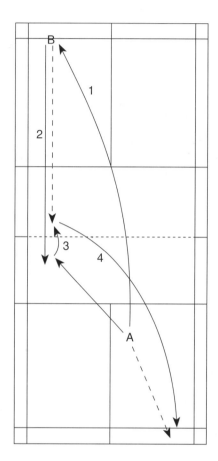

Success Goal = 3 three-shot rallies out of 4 attempts in succession ___

Success Check
- Hit clears high and deep ___
- Hit smashes downward with some pace ___
- Let drop shots fall close to the top of the net ___

6. Crosscourt Three-Shot Continuous Rally

Player A begins the rally with an underhand clear to Player B's deep forehand corner. Player B returns this clear with a crosscourt drop shot or smash to Player A's forehand at the net. Player A returns this net drop shot with a straight ahead net drop shot. Player B then clears deep to Player A's deep forehand corner, and they repeat the three-shot sequence: clear, drop/smash, drop.

Success Goal = 3 three-shot rallies out of 4 attempts in succession ___

Success Check
- Hit clears high and deep ___
- Hit smashes downward with some pace ___
- Let drop shots fall close to the top of the net ___

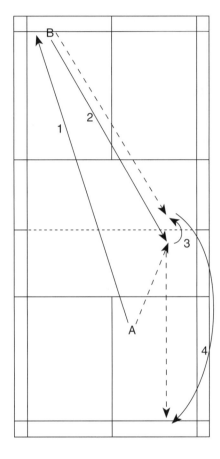

7. Six-Shooter Footwork Rally

Player C is stationed in backcourt and begins the rally by clearing to Player B's deep forehand court. Player B hits a forehand overhead clear straight ahead to Player C's deep backhand. Player C hits a crosscourt drop to Player B's left frontcourt. Player B re-drops with a spin or tumble net drop shot. Player A, stationed at the net, immediately hits the net drop shot with a quick, flat return to Player B's deep right backcourt. Player B clears out of her right backcourt. This sequence forces you to move quickly, even more quickly than you would like to, in order to cover the singles' court.

Success Goal = 2 out of 3 successful attempts ___

Success Check
- Hit clears high and deep ___
- Let drop shots tumble and fall close to the top of the net ___
- Hit drive shots quickly and flat ___

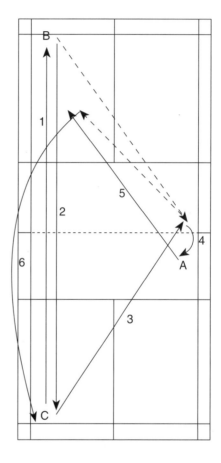

8. Box of 50

A box of 50 shuttles is placed in a chair, on a table, or held by a third player on one side of your court near the "T". Player A begins with 8 to 12 shuttles held in one hand and throws one shuttle at a time over the net to Player B. Player B may hit any return other than a clear. His primary objective is to get the shuttle on the floor as soon as possible. In addition, Player B must try to recover to center court after each shot. Therefore, Player A must pause slightly between throws to give Player B enough time to recover. However, you can make the drill progressively more difficult by giving less and less time between throws. This speeding up of the throws forces Player B to move more quickly and serves as a good means of physical conditioning. Even if Player B misses or fails to reach a return, Player A should continue until all the shuttles have been thrown.

Success Goal = complete the Box of 50 with less than 10 total misses or errors ___

Success Check
• Use proper footwork ___

To Increase Difficulty
• Give less time between throws.

To Decrease Difficulty
• Give more time between throws.

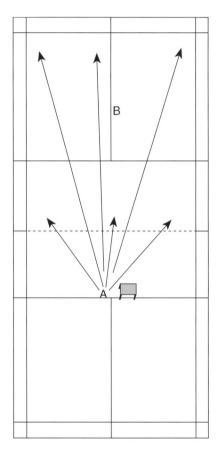

9. Six-Shot Rallies

These drills emphasize your stroke production, that is, the choice of your return from various locations on your court during any rally or point. The following will illustrate three six-shot drills that you may use to practice your strokes. You may also practice them beginning from the right or left side of your court. Where you begin necessarily places more emphasis on your forehand or your backhand returns.

- ■ (a) straight clear; (b) straight return clear; (c) crosscourt clear; (d) straight return clear; (e) crosscourt drop shot; and (f) net drop shot
- ■ (a) straight clear; (b) crosscourt drop shot; (c) net drop shot return; (d) crosscourt drive or push; (e) straight clear; and (f) crosscourt smash
- ■ (a) crosscourt clear; (b) crosscourt smash; (c) net shot; (d) crosscourt clear; (e) straight clear; and (f) straight smash
- ■ (a) crosscourt clear; (b) crosscourt drop shot; (c) net shot; (d) crosscourt clear; (e) straight smash; and (f) crosscourt drive

Success Goal = 3 six-shot rallies out of 4 attempts in succession ___

Success Check
- Hit clears high and deep ___
- Hit smashes downward with some pace ___
- Let drop shots fall close to the top of the net ___
- Hit drive shots quickly and in a flat trajectory ___

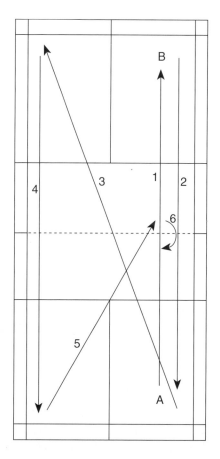

10. Modified Singles

The playing area of the singles' court is reduced to the areas shown. Players may use only clears and drop shots to win rallies and points. Keep your score just as in normal singles' play.

Success Goal = most returns fall into target, shaded areas ___

Success Check
• Use proper footwork ___
• Hit clears high and deep ___
• Let drop shots fall close to the top of the net ___

SINGLES' PLAY SUCCESS SUMMARY

You cannot plan a specific strategy for every possible situation. However, there are general principles that you can apply to almost every singles' game plan or strategy, particularly as your skill level increases:

■ Play to your strengths and to your opponent's weaknesses.
■ Force your opponent into making errors by being very consistent and steady.
■ Keep your opponent moving.
■ Change the pace during play.
■ Never change a winning strategy; always change a losing strategy.
■ Try to make all your overhead strokes look the same; deception is a key part of becoming a better player.

Practice until your singles' play results in an effective, accurate, and successful stroke production. When you are ready, ask a coach or instructor to observe you and check your stroke production during actual singles' game play. Attempt to visualize each stroke and critique your shot selection with your evaluator following the match.

STEP 10
DOUBLES' PLAY: ROTATION AND TEAMWORK

Doubles is very different from singles, primarily because you now have a partner, but also because you usually have less time to think and react. Your doubles' tactics are greatly dependent upon your court position. You will probably enjoy doubles' play and have more success if you learn to rotate and play as a team. The rotational system consists of you and your partner rotating from an up and back position to a side-by-side position, depending on whether you are on offense or defense. The team on offense supposedly has the shuttle directed downward, and they will change to a side-by-side or defending position when either partner is forced to hit the shuttle upward.

Starting in and maintaining the correct court position are essential to successful doubles' play. An important element of this principle involves trusting your partner during the rally. Allow him to make his own shots. You should hit serves and returns during any doubles' rally with the objective of forcing your opponents to lift to you or your partner.

Men's, women's, and mixed doubles require the same strokes, techniques, teamwork, and strategy to be successful. In normal doubles' play, both the server and the receiver play close to the net and their partners are temporarily responsible for the backcourt. The initial stroke by either team is one to maneuver their opponents into a position that requires them to lift their returns. The subsequent misdirection or jockeying for the offensive position usually determines which team wins the rally.

Doubles' play in badminton is enjoyable for many reasons. It is a great recreational game that you can enjoy socially and competitively. It allows you to practice teamwork and strategy. Doubles' play also gets your heart beating faster, requires that you move quickly, and makes you think on your feet. This mental practice and physical activity possibly aid in allowing you to relax, relieving stress, and providing some physical conditioning. Badminton doubles is a game that you can play throughout your life.

How to Position Yourself and Play As a Team in Doubles

Your position in doubles to a great extent determines the type of return that you or your partner will make and how effectively you will both be able to get to your opponents' return. Figure 10.1 shows the beginning position for both teams as you deliver your serve. Both the server and the receiver are trying to get their opponents to lift the shuttle up to them or to their partners. Initially, both teams are vying for the offensive position, so they both start up and back. Because you can only score when you are serving, it is necessary to develop an accurate and consistent low serve while standing as close to the short service line and the centerline as possible. The drive and flick serves may give your opponents a different look and keep them more honest while they are receiving the serve. You can use either the forehand or backhand serving motion effectively. Because the low serve is used most often, it is important to hit a safe, conservative return of serve that will keep your opponents honest and cause them to lift your return.

One of the following three choices of returns should be successful: (1) a push shot, (2) a midcourt drive, or (3) a net drop shot. Direct the midcourt drive or push shot past the partner at the net to cause the back partner to contact the shuttle low and force him or her to lift the shuttle upward. However, if the partner who is up does not play aggressively toward the net after serving, then a hairpin or tumble drop shot at the net should force him or her to hit the shuttle up. The half court drive or push return is your best overall answer to a good serve. Half court returns and drives are the safest choices during men's, women's, and mixed doubles' play. The main objectives are to keep the shuttle going downward, gain the offensive position, and keep it. Figures 10.2 and 10.3 illustrate the rotational system of doubles' court coverage.

The side-by-side formation provides a better defense and allows you and your partner to more easily return any of your opponents' shots that are hit downward. The up and back system is preferable for your team when you have the shuttle going down into your opponents' court or when your opponents are forced to hit upward. The rotational system, in which you change from being up and back to being side by side, allows transition between rallies. There are times when you or your partner must lift or clear the shuttle. In this case, you should shift to the side-by-side formation. If you or your partner is able to hit a return downward and force your opponents to lift the shuttle, then you should shift into the up and back formation. Another example of shifting to the up and back formation would be on a high serve delivered to you or your partner. As soon as the high serve is delivered to your partner, change places.

From his up position receiving the serve, he moves back to return the high serve. And from your back position straddling the centerline, you move to the net and to prepare for any net returns from your partner's downward return of serve. The same is true in reverse, when either you or your partner initiates a high serve. When a high serve is delivered from the server's up position, she rotates back into the side-by-side formation. As soon as you recognize your partner's high serve, you move opposite your partner to cover the other side.

Other general strategies for doubles' play are:

- Always try to hit the shuttle downward, even if from lack of speed.
- When serving, serve the low, short serve most of the time.
- When serving, play aggressively toward the net. Absolutely prevent your opponents from hitting drop shots.
- When receiving, get as close as possible to the net, but always be thinking "long serve." Push or misdirect most returns past the up partner.
- When smashing, smash straight ahead most of the time.
- Get the shuttle over the net as soon as possible. A straight net drop shot is usually preferable to one hit crosscourt, unless your opponent is directly in front of you across the net.

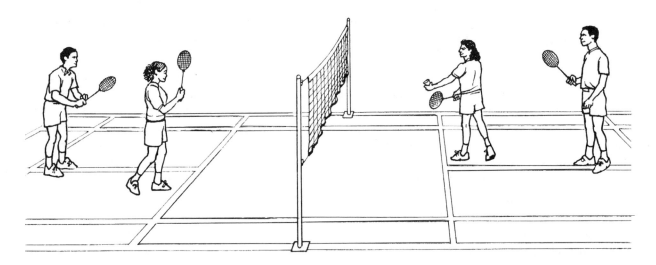

Figure 10.1   Beginning positions for doubles players.

Figure 10.2 Doubles positions following service return.

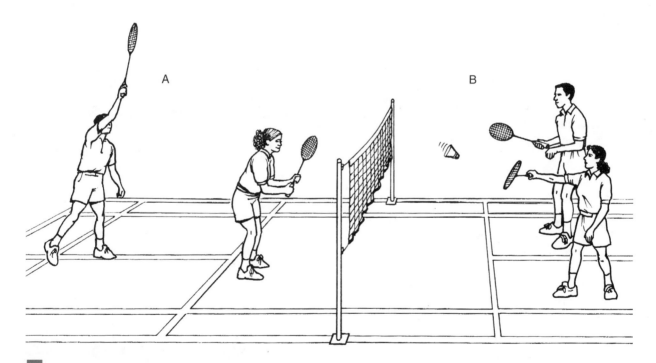

Figure 10.3 Doubles positions after clear and smash return. Team A is on offense, up and back; Team B is on defense, side by side.

DOUBLES' PLAY SUCCESS STOPPERS

In doubles' play, it is much more difficult to hit the shuttle away from both of your opponents. If you hit it away from one partner, you are essentially hitting it to the other. You must be able to serve low and short to your opponents successfully. Never attempt to direct the shuttle upward during a rally. Partners trying to cover too much court or trying to make all the shots may create problems. Avoid criticizing or blaming your partner for mistakes or missed shots.

Error	Correction
1. You lack confidence or success on your short serve.	1. Practice your short serve with both forehand and backhand deliveries.
2. Partners do not cooperate or try to complement each other's strengths and weaknesses.	2. Work together. You should discuss strategy, strengths, weaknesses, and court coverage before play.
3. You lack strategy.	3. Cooperate and communicate. Help each other by calling birds out during rallies and on short or long serves. Play the bird to the weaker of your opponents.
4. You lack communication during play.	4. Discuss specific game situations in advance, before playing.
5. You have indecision about who should make the return.	5. Try to consistently be in proper position. The partner who has the shuttle on her forehand should hit returns down the middle.
6. Too many of your returns are hit upward.	6. When in doubt, smash!

DOUBLES' PLAY

DRILLS

1. Doubles' Short Serve-Push Return

Player A serves short to Player B. Player B returns this short serve with a push return to her partner's backhand or forehand side alley. This is not a rally. Player A serves until Player B accomplishes five good returns toward her backhand or forehand side alley. This pushed return should carry beyond her partner's short service line. After five good returns have been made, Player B should serve short to Player A and allow her to make five good push returns of serve.

**Success Goal** = 30 good push returns by each player ___

✔ **Success Check**
• Serves cross over close to top of net ___
• Push returns travel to near midcourt, past short service line ___

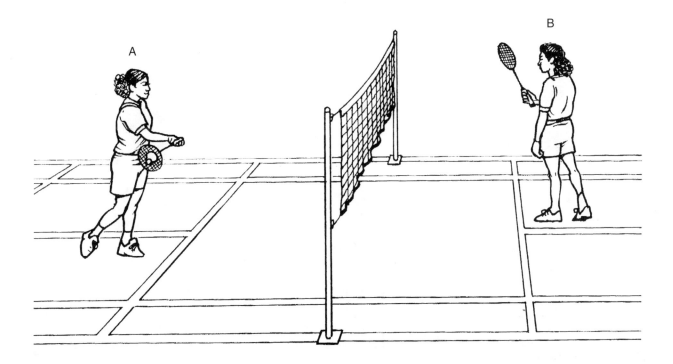

2. Doubles' Short Serve-Net Drop Shot

Player A serves short to Player B. Player B returns this short serve with a drop shot at the net to her partner's backhand side alley or returns this short serve with a net drop shot return to her partner's forehand side alley. This is not a rally. Player A serves until Player B accomplishes five good returns toward her backhand or forehand side alley. This pushed return should carry into her partner's backhand side alley to be considered a good return. After five good returns have been made, Player B should serve short to Player A and allow her to make five good net drop shot returns of serve to her backhand.

Success Goal = 30 good drop shot returns by each player ___

Success Check
* Serves cross over close to top of net ___
* Drop shot returns travel close to net and fall toward floor ___

To Increase Difficulty
* Tumble drop shot returns instead of bumping or lifting them over.

3. Wide Doubles' Short Serve Drill

Player A serves wide and short to Player B. Player B returns this forehand short serve with a straight ahead drop shot at the net to his partner's forehand and backhand side alleys. This is not a rally. Player A serves until Player B accomplishes five good returns toward his forehand. Then repeat to his backhand side alley. These drop shot returns should carry into his partner's backhand side alley and short of the short service line to be considered good returns. After five good returns of each have been made, players reverse roles and repeat the process. Repeat drill using the short backhand serve.

Success Goal = 30 good drop shot returns from forehand serve by each player ___
30 good drop shot returns from backhand serve by each player ___

To Increase Difficulty
• Tumble drop shot returns instead of bumping or lifting them over.

Success Check
• Serves cross over close to top of net ___
• Serves travel crosscourt and toward alley ___
• Drop shot returns travel close to net and fall toward floor ___

4. *High Serve-Rotate-Smash-Block*

Doubles' Teams A and B are on opposite sides of the net in up and back positions. Player A1 serves high to Player B1. Players A1 and A2 fall into a side-by-side defensive position. Players B1 and B2 change positions. As Player B1 retreats to hit high serve, Player B2 goes to the net. Player B1 hits smash return and either A1 or A2 attempts to return the smash with a block.

Success Goal = 20 good returns by serving team of the smash with block returns ___ 20 good smash returns by the receiving team of the high serve ___

Success Check

- Serving team moves into side-by-side defensive position ___
- Receiving team switches positions to retain up and back offensive position ___

To Increase Difficulty

- Serving team attempts to clear the smash return instead of blocking it.

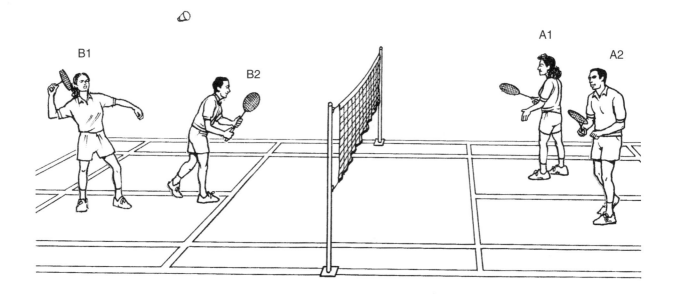

5. Clear-Smash-Block Continuous Rally

Player A begins the rally with an underhand clear approximately midcourt to Player B. Player B smashes straight ahead at Player A, who blocks his partner's smash with a drop shot return or returns his partner's smash with a clear return. Player B then clears to Player A and they repeat the rally.

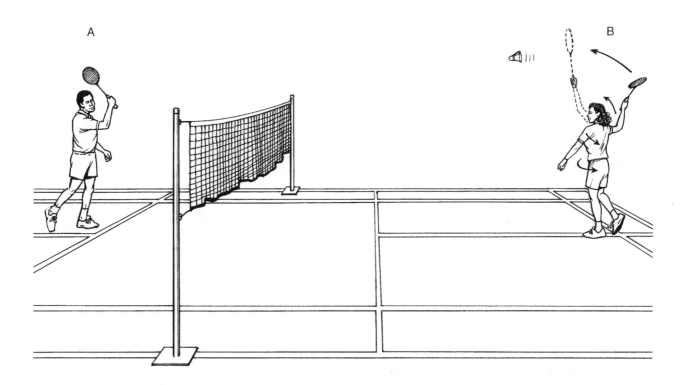

Success Goal = 6 shots in succession without missing ___
30-second rally without missing ___

Success Check
• Smashes travel downward with some power ___
• Block returns stay close to net and fall from lack of power ___
• Clear returns are high and deep ___

6. *Wide Doubles' Serve-Net Shot Rally*

Player B serves wide and short to Player A. Player A returns the serve with a straight ahead net drop shot to the server's backhand side. Player B hits a crosscourt drop to Player A who re-drops to Player C's forehand alley. Player C then crosscourt drops to Player A and the rally continues until one of the three players misses a return. Players B and C only hit crosscourt drop shots. Player A only hits straight net drop shots.

Success Goal = 6 shots in succession without missing ___
30-second rally without missing ___

Success Check
• Serves stay close to top of net ___
• Net drop shot returns travel close to top of net and fall close to net ___

To Increase Difficulty
• Tumble drop shot returns instead of bumping or lifting them over.

7. Short Serve-Push Return Rally

Player A1 serves short to Player B1. Player B1 returns this short serve with a push return to her opponent's backhand side alley or a push return to her opponent's forehand side alley. This is a rally, therefore Player A2 should attempt to return this shot with a push return to Player B2 near midcourt. These pushed midcourt drive returns should carry beyond each partner's short service line and be directed near your opponent's side alley. Players A1 and B1 should remain near the "T" and feint as if trying to intercept the returns being made down the sidelines. After Players A2 and B2 have made an exchange of at least five good returns, both sets of partners should switch places. Player A2 should serve short to Player B2 and allow him to make five good push returns of serve. Players A1 and B1 attempt to rally back and forth down the sidelines.

Success Goal = 6 shots in succession without missing ___
30-second rally without missing ___

Success Check
• Serves stay close to top of net ___
• Push returns travel close to top of net and fall near midcourt ___

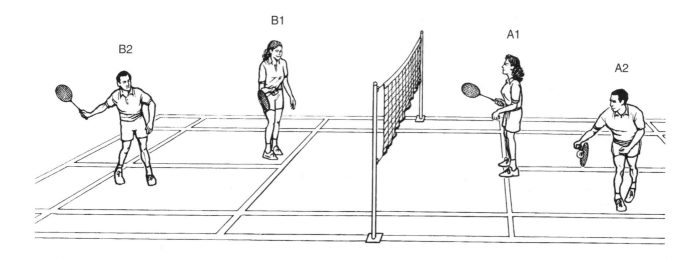

B2   B1   A1   A2

8. Flat Drive Continuous Rally

Player A sets up Player B by hitting a drive to him near midcourt. Player B hits a forehand or backhand drive back and this continues until one of the players misses. Keep these returns at approximately waist high or higher, with a mixture of forehand and backhand exchanges. Emphasize a quick-quick or flat-flat exchange back and forth over the net.

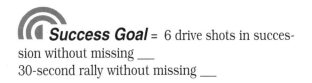**Success Goal** = 6 drive shots in succession without missing ___
30-second rally without missing ___

**Success Check**

• Drives stay close to top of net and travel horizontally ___

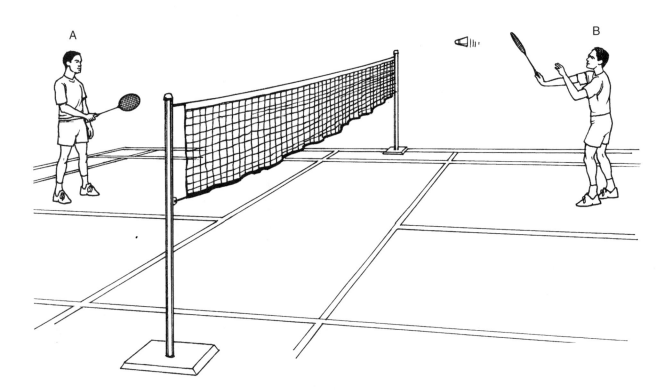

9. Modified Doubles

The playing area of the doubles' court is reduced to the areas shown. Players may use any type of return or shot to win rallies and points. However, after the initial doubles' serve, only the side alleys are in bounds. Otherwise, keep your score just as in normal doubles' play.

Success Goal = most returns fall into target, shaded areas ___

✔ **Success Check**

• Use proper footwork ___
• Partners cover the court with proper formation ___
• Most shots are directed downward and/or fall close to the top of the net ___

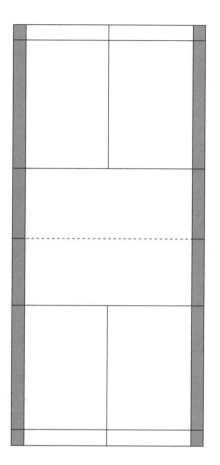

DOUBLES' PLAY SUCCESS SUMMARY

Starting in and maintaining the correct court position are essential to successful doubles' play. An important element of this principle involves trusting your partner during the rally. Allow her to make her own shots. Hit serves and returns during any doubles' rally with the objective of forcing your opponents to lift to you or your partner. Men's, women's, and mixed doubles require the same strokes, techniques, teamwork, and strategy to be successful. In normal doubles' play, both the server and the receiver play close to the net and their partners are temporarily responsible for the backcourt. The initial stroke by either team is to maneuver its opponents into a position that requires them to lift their return. The subsequent misdirection or jockeying for the offensive position usually determines which team wins the rally.

RATING YOUR PROGRESS

Each drill you completed in this book had a success goal, which helped to develop your fundamental skills and strategy for badminton singles' and doubles' play. The following rating chart allows you to rate your overall progress. Rate your success in badminton by writing a number in the space provided to the right of each badminton skill listed. Read each item carefully and respond objectively. Then, review your strengths and weaknesses, and set new goals.

5 = Outstanding 4 = Very good 3 = Fair 2 = Needs extra work 1 = Weakness

FUNDAMENTAL SKILLS

The first general success goal in badminton is to develop the fundamental skills needed to play the game. How would you rate yourself on the fundamental skills? Do you consistently do the following?

Ready Position

Keep your feet square	5	4	3	2	1
Keep your toes straight	5	4	3	2	1
Spread your feet shoulder width	5	4	3	2	1
Keep your knees slightly bent	5	4	3	2	1
Keep your weight on balls of feet	5	4	3	2	1
Hold your racket up in front of body	5	4	3	2	1
Hold your racket with handshake grip	5	4	3	2	1
Keep your eyes on shuttle	5	4	3	2	1

Footwork

Watch bird and opponent	5	4	3	2	1
Lead with dominant foot	5	4	3	2	1
Pivot on nondominant foot	5	4	3	2	1
Reach with dominant arm or leg	5	4	3	2	1
Shuffle or step-close-step	5	4	3	2	1
Cross over only on backhands	5	4	3	2	1
Recover to ready position	5	4	3	2	1
Keep your balance	5	4	3	2	1

Serves

Have correct starting stance	5	4	3	2	1
Have correct position on court	5	4	3	2	1
Transfer your weight into serve	5	4	3	2	1

Use forearm rotation and wrist action	5	4	3	2	1
Make contact below waist	5	4	3	2	1
Execute your long serve	5	4	3	2	1
Execute your forehand short serve	5	4	3	2	1
Execute your backhand short serve	5	4	3	2	1
Execute your drive serve	5	4	3	2	1
Execute your flick serve	5	4	3	2	1

Knowledge

Know the history of badminton	5	4	3	2	1
Know the rules of badminton	5	4	3	2	1
Understand how to keep score	5	4	3	2	1
Learn by watching	5	4	3	2	1

Mental Preparation

Have desire and persistence	5	4	3	2	1
Have motivation to come from behind	5	4	3	2	1
Have concentration and ability to block out noise	5	4	3	2	1
Use mental practice such as visual imagery	5	4	3	2	1

Forehand Stroke

Have correct grip and ready position	5	4	3	2	1
Move into your hitting stance	5	4	3	2	1
Transfer your weight into shot	5	4	3	2	1
Use forearm pronation and wrist action	5	4	3	2	1
Execute your clear	5	4	3	2	1
Execute your drop shot	5	4	3	2	1
Execute your smash	5	4	3	2	1
Execute your drive	5	4	3	2	1
Execute your around the head stroke	5	4	3	2	1

Backhand Stroke

Have correct grip and ready position	5	4	3	2	1
Move into your hitting stance	5	4	3	2	1
Transfer your weight into shot	5	4	3	2	1
Use forearm supination and wrist action	5	4	3	2	1
Execute your clear	5	4	3	2	1
Execute your drop shot	5	4	3	2	1
Execute your smash	5	4	3	2	1
Execute your drive	5	4	3	2	1

Total your score for your fundamental skills. A general indication of your skills would be as follows:

Excellent	200 or more points
Good	145-199 points
Fair	100-144 points
Poor	99 or fewer points

YOUR SCORE: _____

SINGLES' AND DOUBLES' STRATEGY

The second general success goal in badminton is to develop your ability to play singles and doubles. This includes making correct choices regarding your tactics while playing points, communicating with and complementing your partner in doubles, and covering the court as a team. How would you rate your abilities in the following aspects of singles' and doubles' play? Are you able to do the following?

Singles' Tactics

Analyze your strengths	5	4	3	2	1
Recognize your weaknesses	5	4	3	2	1
Analyze your opponent's strengths	5	4	3	2	1
Recognize your opponent's weaknesses	5	4	3	2	1
Have patience during rallies	5	4	3	2	1
Play safely, more conservatively when receiving	5	4	3	2	1
Play aggressively when serving	5	4	3	2	1
Make rallies last if your opponent lacks endurance	5	4	3	2	1
Know the boundaries of singles' court	5	4	3	2	1
Train harder if you lack endurance	5	4	3	2	1
Recover to center court	5	4	3	2	1
Anticipate your opponent's returns	5	4	3	2	1
Hit to your opponent's backhand	5	4	3	2	1
Remain alert	5	4	3	2	1
Make good decisions in shot selection	5	4	3	2	1
Be mentally tough	5	4	3	2	1
Consistently get in position to make line calls	5	4	3	2	1
Don't complain about your opponent's line calls	5	4	3	2	1
Utilize the clear and drop shot to move your opponent	5	4	3	2	1

Doubles' Tactics

Analyze your strengths	5	4	3	2	1
Recognize your weaknesses	5	4	3	2	1
Analyze your opponents' strengths	5	4	3	2	1
Recognize your opponents' weaknesses	5	4	3	2	1
Cooperate with your partner	5	4	3	2	1
Complement each other during play	5	4	3	2	1
Demonstrate good sportsmanship	5	4	3	2	1
Don't criticize, complain, or blame your partner	5	4	3	2	1
Play aggressively; attack at every opportunity	5	4	3	2	1
Learn rotational system for covering court	5	4	3	2	1
Learn doubles' boundary lines	5	4	3	2	1
Hit down middle to cause indecision	5	4	3	2	1
Try not to cover too much court	5	4	3	2	1
Try not to make all the shots	5	4	3	2	1
Smash or hit down at every opportunity	5	4	3	2	1
Anticipate your opponent's returns	5	4	3	2	1

Remain alert	5	4	3	2	1
Make good decisions in shot selection	5	4	3	2	1
Be mentally tough	5	4	3	2	1

Total your score for a general indication of your tactics in singles' and doubles' play. Your rating scale would be as follows:

Excellent	140 or more points
Good	105-139 points
Fair	70-104 points
Poor	69 or fewer points

YOUR SCORE: _____

For a more comprehensive comparison of your current skill level, total both of the previous areas and compare as follows:

Excellent	340 or more points
Good	250-339 points
Fair	170-249 points
Poor	169 or fewer points

TOTAL SCORE: _____

Now look back at your self-ratings for each badminton skill. What does this tell you about your areas of strengths and weaknesses? What goals would you prepare for yourself to increase your badminton skills and future enjoyment?

GLOSSARY

alley—Playing area that comes into or out of play at various times during any game. For example, the side alley is the playing area on each side of the court between the singles' sideline and the doubles' sideline. This 1.5-foot (0.46 meter) wide area is in play for doubles, but out of bounds for singles. The back alley is an area 2.5 feet (0.76 meters) deep between the doubles' back service line and the back boundary line. It is out of bounds on any doubles' serve. After the serve is in play, this alley is in bounds for any other return.

around the head stroke—A return made with your forehand but contacted over your nondominant shoulder.

back boundary line—The line similar to the baseline in tennis that designates the end or back of the badminton playing area.

backcourt—Approximately the last 11 feet (3.35 meters) of the court on any side of the net or midcourt to the back boundary line.

backhand—Any return or stroke hit on the nondominant side of the body.

backhand grip—The manner in which you grasp your racket to hit any return from your nondominant side. In badminton, this is usually done with the handshake or pistol grip, held with your dominant thumb in an up position on the top left side of the handle.

backswing—That part of the swing that takes the racket back in preparation for the forward swing.

base—A spot near the middle of your court that you should try to return to after most shots.

baseline—The line designating the back boundary of your court.

bird—The missile or object struck with the badminton racket that begins the rally over the net. Same as shuttle or shuttlecock.

carry—A return that is caught on the racket face and is slung or thrown over the net. It is sometimes referred to as a sling or a throw. This is a legal return as long as it is a continuation of your normal stroke and is not a double hit.

clear—A high return that carries deep into the backcourt.

crosscourt—A return or stroke that sends the bird diagonally across the court.

double hit—This occurs when the shuttle is hit twice in succession on the same stroke. A fault.

doubles' service court—This is the serving area into which the doubles' serve must be delivered. Each side of a badminton court has a right and a left service court for doubles. Each doubles' service court is bounded by the short service line, the centerline, the doubles' sideline, and the doubles' back service line. Its dimensions are 13 feet (3.96 meters) long by 10 feet (3.05 meters) wide. It is sometimes referred to as short and fat. The side alley is in bounds; the back alley is not.

drive—A return or stroke that sends the shuttle in a relatively flat trajectory, parallel to the floor, but high enough to pass over the net.

drive serve—A hard, fast serve that crosses the net with a flat trajectory and is usually directed toward the receiver's nondominant shoulder. It is used more in doubles than in singles.

drop shot—A return or stroke that barely clears the net and falls toward the floor, hit underhand or overhand from the net or the backcourt.

fault—Any violation of the rules.

flick serve or flick return—An especially quick, flat serve or return initiated by a flick of the wrist that loops the bird high out of reach toward the rear of your opponent's court. It is used primarily in doubles if your opponent is consistently rushing your serve.

follow-through—The smooth continuation of a stroke after your racket has contacted the bird.

forehand—Any return or stroke hit on the dominant side of your body.

forehand grip—The manner in which you grasp your racket to hit any return from your dominant side. The handshake or pistol grip is the most common forehand grip in badminton.

frontcourt—Approximately the front 11 feet (3.35 meters) of the court on any one side of the net or midcourt to the net. The front part of the court, sometimes referred to as the forecourt.

game—A competition that has a goal of a specified number of points. A women's singles' game consists of 11 points; all other games, such as men's singles, men's and women's doubles, and mixed doubles, are played to 15 points.

hairpin drop shot—A form of drop shot played from near the net that travels up one side of the net and down the other side, thus forming a trajectory in the shape of a hairpin.

hands down—This term refers to the partner or partners who have lost their turns at serving. One hand down means one partner has lost his or her serve. Two hands down means both partners have lost their serves, which indicates that their service is over or their side is out. The initial service of any doubles' game begins with one hand down.

inning—An individual's or team's turn at serving or the serving turn on one end of the court.

International Badminton Federation—The I.B.F. is the governing body for badminton play and competition throughout the world.

let—A form of interference in which the point is replayed.

love—In scoring, meaning zero or no points have been scored.

love-all—Zero-all or no points have been scored for either side.

match—A competition that has a specified number of games. In order to win a match, you usually have to win two out of three games.

match point—The point that wins the match.

mixed doubles—A four-handed game in which male and female partners team together to play on opposite sides of the net from each other.

net shot—Any return that strikes the net and continues over into your opponent's court. This might also apply to any drop shot return played from a point near the net.

overhead—Any stroke played from a point above head height.

placement—A return hit to a specific spot in your opponent's court where it will be difficult to return.

push shot—A return or shot hit or pushed softly down into your opponent's court. In doubles, this usually means past the opposing partner stationed at the net.

rally—This refers to any exchange back and forth across the net between opposing players during any particular point.

ready position—This is your basic waiting position near center court, which is equidistant from all corners. This position affords you the best opportunity to get to any possible return made by your opponent.

receiver—Any player who receives the serve.

return—Any method of hitting your opponent's shots back over the net.

serve or service—The act of putting the shuttle into play at the beginning of a point or rally.

server—The player who delivers the serve.

service court—One of the two half courts divided by the net into which the serve must be directed. There are right and left service courts for singles' and doubles' play. They differ in size and shape.

service over—Loss of your serve, serve goes over to your opponent.

setting—Method of extending a tie game unique to badminton. Game points are increased when the score is tied at 9-all or 10-all in women's singles' play or at 13-all or 14-all in doubles' and men's singles' play. Instead of playing to 11, women's singles' game point can be extended to 12 in both cases. Instead of playing to 15, the 13-all tie may be extended 5 points to 18, and the 14-all tie may be extended to 3 additional points or to 17. The option of setting is determined by the player or team who reaches the tie score first.

short service line—This is the front line designating the beginning of the service court and is situated 6 feet and 6 inches (1.98 meters) from the net.

shuttle or shuttlecock—The missile used in badminton. Same as bird.

side out—Loss of your service. Same as service over or two hands down in doubles' play.

singles' service court—This is the serving area into which the singles' serve must be delivered. Each side of a badminton court has a right and a left service court for singles. Each singles' service court is bounded by the short service line, the centerline, the singles' sideline and the back boundary line. Its dimensions are 15.5 feet (5.03 meters) long by 8.5 feet (2.59 meters) wide. It is sometimes referred to as long and narrow.

singles' sideline—The singles' sideline designates the out of bounds for singles' play. The singles' court is 17 feet wide (5.18 meters) from sideline to sideline.

smash—An overhead return or stroke hit down into your opponents' court with great speed and power.

stroke—The act of hitting the bird with your racket.

Thomas Cup—This is men's international badminton team competition similar to the Davis Cup in tennis. It was first held in 1948. Six singles' and three doubles' matches are played between two countries. Thomas Cup competition is held on a two-year cycle in the even years.

Uber Cup—The Uber Cup is a women's international team competition. It began in 1957 and was named for a former English player, Mrs. H.S. Uber. It is also held on a two-year cycle in the even years.

United States Badminton Association—The U.S.B.A. is the national governing body for badminton in the United States of America. The U.S.B.A. was formerly the American Badminton Association from 1936 until 1977, when it was reorganized and renamed.

wood shot—This return or shot results from the tip or cork of the shuttle hitting on the frame of your racket rather than on the strings. Although it has not always been a legal return, the I.B.F. ruled in 1963 that wood shots were acceptable.

SUGGESTED READINGS

Ballou, Ralph B. *Badminton for Beginners.* Englewood, Colo.: Morton, 1992.

Bloss, Margaret Varner, and R. Stanton Hales. *Badminton.* 6th ed. Dubuque, Iowa: Brown, 1990.

Breen, James, and Donald Paup. *Winning Badminton.* North Palm Beach, Fla.: Athletic Institute, 1983.

Davidson, Kenneth, and Leland Gustavson. *Winning Badminton.* rev. ed. Melbourne, Fla.: Krieger, 1964.

Hales, Diane. "A History of Badminton in the United States from 1878-1939." Master's thesis, California Polytechnic University, 1979.

Lo, Diana, and Kevin Stark. "The Badminton Overhead Shot." *National Strength and Conditioning Association Journal* 13, 4 (1991): 6-13 and 87-89.

Poole, James. *Badminton.* 3rd ed. Springfield, Ill.: Scott-Foresman, 1982.

Rogers, Wynn. *Advanced Badminton.* Dubuque, Iowa: Brown, 1970.

Wadood, Tariq, and Karlyne Tan. *Badminton Today.* St. Paul: West, 1990.

ABOUT THE AUTHOR

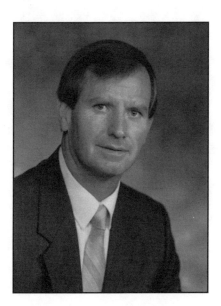

Tony Grice, who has been playing and coaching badminton nationally and internationally since 1975, has been ranked as 11th nationwide in men's doubles and 15th in men's singles. He has taught and coached the sport at both the high school and college levels.

Tony has been a board member and national team exercise physiologist for the U.S. Badminton Association (USBA). He traveled with the U.S. National Badminton Team to the 1987 World Championships in Beijing as team trainer. Two years later he was manager for the South Team at the 1989 Olympic Sports Festival in Oklahoma City, and he was official umpire at the 1993 Olympic Festival in San Antonio. He holds USBA certification as a Level III national coach and regional umpire.

Tony has taught badminton at Northwestern State University in Louisiana, the University of Texas at Austin, and Texas A&M University, where he served as coordinator of racquet sports. He has also conducted numerous badminton instructional clinics in the United States, Guatemala, and Mexico.

In addition to working with the 1996 Olympic Badminton Team, Tony continues to teach a badminton class each semester at Hardin-Simmons University in Abilene, Texas, where he is a professor in the Physical Education Department and director of the Aerobic-Human Performance Laboratory.

Tony received his BS and MEd degrees from Memphis State University and an EdD from Northwestern State University in Louisiana. He resides in Abilene with his wife, Kristen, and in his spare time enjoys playing badminton, tennis, and golf.

Other books in the
Steps to Success Activity Series

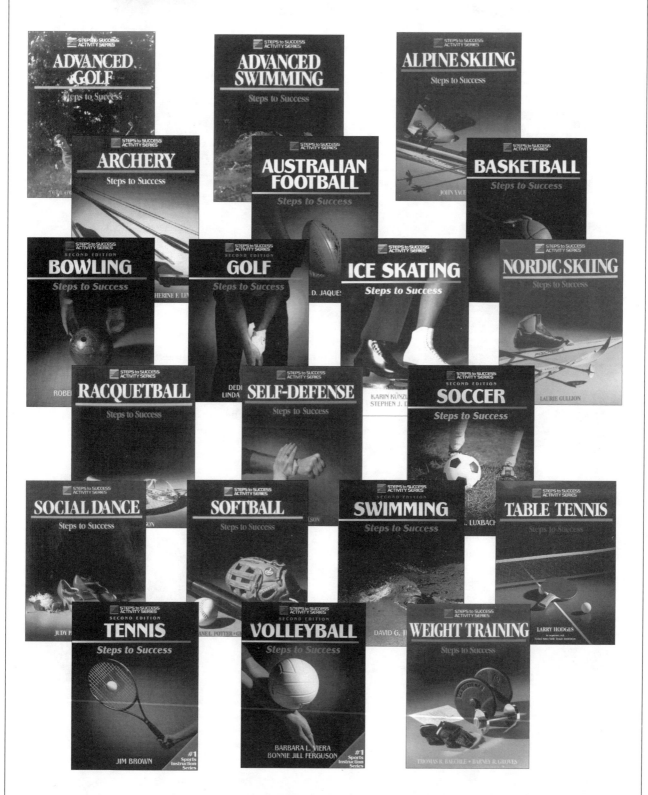

Improve Your Training Skills

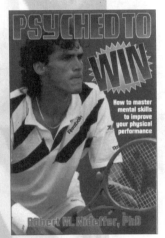